DANCING

in

SMALL
SPACES

DANCING

in

SMALL SPACES

One Couple's Journey with
Parkinson's Disease and Lewy Body Dementia

Leslie A. Davidson

BRINDLE
AND GLASS

Brindle & Glass

An imprint of TouchWood Editions

touchwoodeditions.com

Edited by Kate Kennedy

Copy edited by Meg Yamamoto

Cover and interior design by Sydney Barnes

Cover photo by Martin Gidney. All other photos are from the author's collection.

CATALOGUING DATA AVAILABLE FROM LIBRARY AND ARCHIVES CANADA

ISBN 9781990071089 (softcover)

ISBN 9781990071096 (electronic)

TouchWood Editions acknowledges that the land on which we live and work is within the traditional territories of the Lkwungen (Esquimalt and Songhees), Malahat, Pacheedaht, Scia'new, T'Sou-ke, and W̱SÁNEĆ (Pauquachin, Tsartlip, Tsawout, Tseycum) peoples.

We acknowledge the financial support of the Government of Canada through the Canada Book Fund and the Canada Council for the Arts, and of the Province of British Columbia through the British Columbia Arts Council and the Book Publishing Tax Credit.

This book was produced using FSC®-certified, acid-free papers, processed chlorine free, and printed with soya-based inks.

Printed in Canada

26 25 24 23 22   1 2 3 4 5

For Lincoln, Sarah, and Naomi. How did I get so lucky?

Prelude

I SIT IN A QUIET ROOM and stare out the window at straight, tall conifers and mountains so close they seem contrived, like set pieces placed by some giant hand, without thought of restraint or reality. Snow has fallen all night long and the mountains are white with the subdued gleam of opals even on this grey morning.

I have been given a gift of time and a beautiful space in which to write, but the trees and the mountains pull my attention from the page. I stare out the window and wonder if he has found his way here with me. Is his eye wandering to peaks and ridges, seeking all the ways through, the best ways up? Is he unfurling maps and tracing thin, curved lines, matching them to all this superfluity of rock and snow, and dreaming of adventures?

I wonder if the raven I could not see but heard this morning, kok-kokking at me—I wonder if that was him? And always, when I think of him, the refrain begins: I miss you. I miss you. I miss you.

This will be about our ending, and because the end is born of a beginning, the beginning shall have a small voice here. I will try to tell the truth of how it was, but I will not tell everything, and there will be poor orderliness in the telling. I know that already. I dig through the memories contained in words I scribbled at the end of bewildering days, in emails sent to friends and family, in the photographs spread on the table and the ones I hold in my mind. I look for patterns, for coherence, for a way to organize the chaos of experience and emotion that was the ending of our together days.

One memory beckons another. Thoughts unfurl, intertwine, reach forward like arms outstretched, grasping at connections more felt than known. What was it I wanted to say?

I stack memories into piles that I label and relabel:

Beginning. Middle. End.
Parkinson's. Dementia.
Grand Forks. Revelstoke.
Family. Friends.
Before. After.
Love. Loss. Grief. Joy.
Guilt. Forgiveness.
Gratitude.
Grace.

I begin to write and lose my way along paths that twist and turn and double back. I cup a memory in the palm of my hand and it shifts, panics, flutters away. I cannot hold it. Thoughts tumble like coloured glass shards in a kaleidoscope, brilliant and transient. Where do they go, these shattered bits of you and me? I talk to myself.

That makes no sense.
It made no sense.

I said that already.
Say it again.

That's too painful to tell.
Tell it anyway.

So many tears.
Yes, so many tears.

Was there really so much laughter?
I think there must have been.

I see myself as an ancient crone, bent and addled, hand-sewing a crazy quilt of all the tattered scraps of our last years. I feather-stitch together the bits and pieces of our stories, and I dream that when it is finished I will wrap it around all those who loved him. We will touch the pieces of ourselves that cling, thread by thread, to one another. I dream we laugh in wonder to be so comforted.

1   More Grateful Than Concerned

I PICK UP A PHOTOGRAPH from the pile on the table. Lincoln.
1977. Though he is not yet my husband, he is already the love of my
life. We have been following the sun through France, then Portugal
and Spain, and finally here to northern Africa. His hair is dark and
curly and he is deeply tanned, and though he is thirty-four years
old, he looks very young. He stands beneath a bright Moroccan sun,
wearing a blue embroidered robe that reaches his bare feet. He feeds
a small group of goats that have gathered round him, stretching their
necks upward toward the bowl of table scraps in his hands.

I hold the photograph and I remember a late morning, the two
of us climbing the winding highway that rises from Agadir and
carves its way high into the Atlas Mountains. A man in a small
black sedan drives up alongside our Volkswagen camper and
waves us down.

"Arrêtez!" he shouts through the open window. "Arrêtez, s'il
vous plaît!"

And so we stop. He is dressed like a Canadian businessman—
white shirt, tie, and a navy suit coat. A fast talker, animated, jovial,
he seems pleased to discover that I have sufficient French to understand that he is Monsieur le Maire, the mayor of the storybook
village we see below us, tucked in against a mountain's flank and
bright with almond blossoms.

"You must come," he says. "We are celebrating! A Berber festival. See!"

He points out long, black tents, some already erected, one just a pile of dark stuff on the ground. I translate for Lincoln, who grins his enthusiasm. We've been together for about eighteen months, long enough for me to expect this delighted response.

"You come," Monsieur le Maire insists. "Spend the night behind the city hall. You will be safe."

We follow his car down the dirt track to the village and park beside a low stucco building within a gated compound. He explains that the gate will be locked for the night.

"You will be safe," he tells us again.

It does not occur to me that we might not be safe. Morocco is a poor country; parts of it are very poor. Travellers like us are, by comparison, members of a wealthy, privileged elite. We've met tourists who have been robbed, usually by pickpockets in the cities or by someone breaking into their vehicles, but none who have been threatened physically. We've been careful about where we camp, and two months into our three-month stay in the country, we have enjoyed only positive encounters with the locals. They are as curious about Canada as we are about Morocco. They ask about our forests, our mountains, and our snow. We absorb lessons on Arabic phrases, food preparation, and even how to avoid giving offence. We have been invited into a number of homes to share meals and, once, into a one-room school to watch student skits and musical performances. This little village and its enthusiastic mayor seem another serendipitous opportunity to experience Moroccan generosity.

Monsieur le Maire watches, intrigued, as we raise the roof of the van, and the canvas half-tent that accommodates our sleeping loft appears. Then he pokes his head into the interior and opens a few cupboards.

"Very nice," he says.

"Will you join us?" I ask. "I'm going to make lunch."

"Non, non, not possible," he says, patting his belly. "I have eaten and I'm very busy."

Then he bustles off in the direction of the building. Soon we find ourselves wandering among the tents. They are handwoven black wool with red and orange geometric designs worked into the borders. Berber women in long, colourful dresses drive wooden stakes into the ground with huge mallets, securing the tents against the mountain winds. They are strong and bold and laughing and I love them instantly. A woman takes my hand and leads me toward a tent as Lincoln is swept up by a chattering group. Once inside, we sink into layers of carpets. They offer pastries and fruit and motion to us to eat. A tiny child with henna-red hair crawls into my lap. A cherub in a striped djellaba. I wear jeans, a denim shirt, and Moroccan leather slippers, the kind men wear, with soles made of rubber from old tires. When Henna Baby gives my breasts a couple of squeezes, the women shriek with laughter. They point from me to Lincoln, to their dresses, to my jeans, to my short hair and their own long hair. I finally understand they are telling me that Henna Baby is confused about my gender. When the child soaks my lap with pee, I hold him up, high and close to me, while his chubby feet puppet-dance in the air. I want to spare the beautiful carpets and I do not mind the pee. I would not change anything about that afternoon.

That night, in our parking spot behind the city hall, we sip mint tea and watch through the open side door of the camper as stars glitter in an ebony sky and Joan Baez sings "Diamonds and Rust" on our tape player. Suddenly, Monsieur le Maire appears out of the darkness, framed in the doorway. Lit by our lantern's glow, he pauses for effect, like Muhammad Ali entering the ring. He grins and flashes silver teeth at each of us before clambering in and squeezing onto the bench seat beside me. He refuses our offer of tea but insists I translate the song lyrics. I have barely begun when he leaps up.

"Dansez avec moi!" he demands and pulls me to my feet.

I look to Lincoln for help but he leans back and smiles. Taking my cue from him, I tell myself this is weird but not dangerous. Surely not dangerous. Monsieur grabs me around the waist and thrusts his pelvis into mine.

"Baisez-moi," he whispers, as we move awkwardly around the four square feet of floor.

"Pardon?"

"Baisez-moi!"

I push myself away and Lincoln sits up straight. He is no longer smiling.

"Non!" I say.

"Pourquoi, non?" Monsieur pouts, pretending to be hurt. Or not pretending.

"Because I am married!"

"You are married?" He sounds angry.

Lincoln stands in response to his change in tone. There are three of us now bumping about in the tiny space, and someone's head jostles the gas-fuelled lantern suspended from the roof.

We are all going to die, I think. The lantern will fall and explode and we will burn and my family will never know what happened to me.

"You have no ring!" he accuses.

"I don't wear it when we travel," I lie.

"Married? Vraiment? Avec papiers?"

"Yes, yes," I lie again. "Avec papiers."

Oh God! What if he wants to see our passports? But he doesn't. He leaves. As abruptly as he came, he leaves. I quickly lock all the doors.

"What if he comes back . . . with friends?"

"What friends?" Lincoln laughs.

And then he climbs into the loft and falls asleep while I spend the night rigidly upright on the seat below, wrapped in a blanket and startling at every small sound. But Monsieur does not come back and we never see him again. I doze off and wake to the dawn and the gate open. Within minutes we are on the road. It is hours before I allow Lincoln to stop to eat and days before I forgive him for not even imagining the horror of what might have been.

"Babe," he says, "nothing happened."

"It could have!"

"But it didn't. I don't understand why you're so upset."

"Because you won't take it seriously."

"Take what seriously?" He is truly puzzled. "Nothing happened."

Round and round and round.

In time, Lincoln's good nature calms me, and Morocco fills my anxious brain with happier pictures. In time, Monsieur le Maire and his silver teeth and his "Baisez-moi" become just another travel story. In time, everything changes.

If a cat walks across the wedding cake, is it a sign? If it is a sign, what does it mean? If it isn't a black cat, that's good, right? Surely a sweet grey kitten can only confer blessings, that is, if one is inclined toward the superstitious. I don't think I am. I know Lincoln isn't. Yet on the morning of our wedding day, we both giggle a little nervously as we scrape away at the icing on the slab cake we plan to serve our guests in a couple of hours. We are removing the stepped-on bits, the places that show where our kitten strolled just minutes before, leaving unmistakable paw prints in the white icing, like tracks in the snow. Our labours remove the evidence of the cat walk but leave the icing thin in places, a problem we solve by rearranging a few decorative silver leaves and adding some fresh flowers. It's a good thing this is an informal wedding—only two weeks in the planning—a potluck celebration with few guests. We plan to serve the cake with strategically placed balls of ice cream. No one is likely to notice our repair job.

My siblings and their partners, two babes in arms, one five-year-old, a couple of old friends, a couple of new friends, Lincoln's mom and dad—that's it, that's the guest list. My parents are far away in Ottawa and can't make the trip on such short notice. I think I am doing them a favour by not expecting their attendance. After all, my first wedding, when I was just twenty-one, the wedding at which my father officiated and for which my mother had done all the preparation, that wedding resulted in a marriage that lasted a short three years. I assume they won't mind not having the expense and hassle of the plane trip for such a simple, low-key, second-time-around celebration. Many years later I am sad and sorry to hear from my mother how hurt they were by my mistaken assumption.

"Why didn't you say something, Mom?" I ask.

"You were so happy, honey," she says. "And all your plans were already made. We didn't want to spoil it for you."

After our fifteen months of travel in Europe and Morocco, Lincoln and I returned to Canada and to teaching jobs in the Peace

River country in northeastern British Columbia. We've now relocated to the South Coast to be closer to family and to escape the rigours of the long northern winter. I have accepted a job teaching Grade 5 in the town of Sechelt, and Lincoln is already working most days as a substitute teacher. We've been only two months in our new rental home, a little clapboard-and-shingle cottage, part of a complex of four cottages all belonging to one family in a beautiful oceanfront location on the Sechelt Peninsula. From our front bay window, we look out on an Emily Carr world: mist-shrouded mountains, forest-green islands, and an ocean that changes colour with the sky.

"Come see! Come see!" we call to each other.

We watch the birds, mythic and wild—cormorants, herons, and eagles. Sometimes the small puppy heads of seals pop up in the ocean waves, first here and then there, teasing us with quick little glimpses.

"Come see! A whale! It is! I saw it breach!"

Ferries churn their way back and forth, guided by raucous gulls. They dock at the property right next door, connecting us to the Lower Mainland at Horseshoe Bay in West Vancouver.

We step outside and fill our lungs with weedy, fishy, fresh ocean air. We sleep and wake to the steady rumble of waves. Along one side of our cottage, flower beds still bloom with sunny rudbeckia, pink echinacea, and mauve fall asters. There is even a tennis court in good repair, but best of all is our beach, a lovely stretch of coarse sand and ocean-tossed logs.

Fifteen months in a Volkswagen camper van, followed by six months in the dark confines of a one-room bachelor apartment throughout the long Fort St. John winter, have left us revelling in this luxury of space, beauty, and comfort. We call it Hyannis Port North, after the Kennedy family compound on Cape Cod.

The morning is drizzly, so we attend to the business of the day—pledging our troth—inside the cottage. Lincoln's father, a retired United Church minister, performs the simple ceremony. I wear a beige crepe dress and Lincoln wears the Harris tweed jacket we found the year before in a charity shop in Scotland, an open-necked shirt, and his best corduroy trousers. I pick flowers from the garden for a small bridal bouquet. We exchange vows from the order of service that Lincoln's dad suggests and I ask him to also read from Ecclesiastes 3. It begins, "To everything there is a season." I have long loved that Old Testament passage, even before the Byrds popularized it in the song "Turn! Turn! Turn!" It is one of my mother's favourite texts as well.

After we've eaten lunch and, of course, the kitty-marked cake, the rain stops, and we take our wineglasses out onto the beach to toast love and family and friendship. The whole group gathers and we snap pictures in turns, setting up cameras on timers and dashing back to squeeze into place before the shutters click. Lincoln conscientiously takes candid shots of everyone. Well, almost everyone.

"I don't think we have any pictures of just the two of us," he tells me a day or two later. "Does that matter?"

I take a moment to reflect, and at first I am amused. *I guess that's what happens when you have too much fun at your own wedding,* I think to myself. Ours was, perhaps, an unconventional celebration, but the bride-and-groom photo is a tradition I wish we had honoured. And I want a picture to send to my mom and dad.

"Yes," I say. "I think it matters."

He must have known how I would feel, because my kind, brand new husband has a plan. The following Saturday we get dressed up again in our wedding duds. I pick another bouquet of flowers. Lincoln sets up his tripod and takes both indoor and outdoor photos. We laugh and pose and the pictures, when they are printed, delight me.

"They look like us," I say.

Perhaps because we were alone, we appear more relaxed, less hurried than we would have been if we'd had others watching or waiting for us to be finished. Now, over forty years later, the photographs still delight me. Have time and memory conspired to make it all seem more perfect than it truly was? When I think back, that is how I remember that day—as perfect. Joyful, lighthearted, and perfect.

Days will follow that challenge the vows we exchanged but many more, so many more, will affirm them. I decide the kitten walking across the cake is just a funny little thing that happened on our wedding day. If I am wrong and it is an omen, then it foretells a bittersweet truth. Even the happiest of marriages is burdened by the knowledge that, barring extraordinary circumstance, one or the other will be left alone. But who thinks of that on their wedding day?

I don't. Even as Lincoln's dad says "as long as you both shall live," I just want to get to the good part, to shout "I do!" and marry this lovely man.

To everything, there is a season.

Late summer of 2004 finds Lincoln's mom, my sweet mother-in-law, Essie, dying at home of metastatic colon cancer. I am on a sabbatical year, an initiative of our school district that allows teachers to work for four years at three-quarters salary and then take a paid fifth year off. Lincoln has retired. Our two daughters, Sarah and Naomi, are fully grown and on their own, strong and capable and finding their way in the world. I am free to care for Essie with the support of a dedicated team of at-home palliative nurses in Abbotsford, BC. She worries that when she dies, we won't leave the apartment clean enough and the neighbours will gossip.

"I'll scrub every inch with a toothbrush," I tell her. "We'll be able to eat off the floor."

"Good," she sighs.

When serious pain finds her and she can no longer pretend it is nothing, I offer her the medication her doctor has prescribed.

"I don't want those," she says. "They're addictive."

"I can't bear to see you suffering," I say.

"Maybe I should go to the hospital."

"Will you take the pills there?"

Silence.

"I'll take you to the hospital if that's what you want," I tell her, "if you think you'd be more comfortable. But don't you do it for me, because if you're going to be in the hospital, so am I."

"You really think it's okay to take a pill?"

"Oh, Essie, yes, yes, I do. How about just a half to start?"

Within a few minutes, she is resting—calm and smiling.

"Oh, Chook," she whispers. "Thank you for putting me in this lovely place."

Because of the pills she is able to listen to me when I tell her how much I love her, how much we all love her.

"If I'd been able to go shopping for a mother-in-law, I'd have picked you," I say.

It's true. Everyone who knows her adores her. She is our children's beloved Nana. Her life is a lesson in kindness, in service to others, in living simply and joyously. She talks to me of her faith, her happiness at "going home," her sorrow at leaving us behind. I've never pretended to have the kind of faith she has, the kind she wishes I had, but she has always listened without judgement to my poorly expressed spiritual beliefs.

"I don't know about God. I believe in kindness. I believe in love. I believe how we treat others matters more than anything." That's what I tell her.

"That's good enough, Chook," she says.

Lincoln and I are both preacher's kids, though he was past childhood by the time his dad stood in the pulpit and I grew up looking at my father speaking from one and as likely to be quoting Camus or Sartre as the Bible.

Lincoln had a wife before me whom his mother loved, and yet Essie welcomed me with open heart and open arms and she loved me, too. We didn't have her grandchildren baptized, and she asked once and never raised the issue again, whatever it might have cost her. And I am sure it must have cost her.

The time is to come when I will be with Lincoln as he finds his way out of this life and into the whatever-is, wherever it is. I will think of his mom and imagine that she is watching me care for her boy, and I will hope she thinks I am doing a good job. I will think of his mom and how alike she and Lincoln are in bravery and acceptance and how grateful I am that she was his, and she was mine, and for the lessons of her love.

Lincoln's dad, Jim, our Jimmy, left England at the war's end with Essie, four-year-old Lincoln, and two-year-old Christine and settled in Port Dalhousie, Ontario, where he worked as an electrical engineer. Jim was well into his fifties when he packed up his family, travelled across the country, and went back to school to earn a bachelor of divinity degree at the University of British Columbia. Lincoln and his father were on campus at the same time, Jim with a goal of ordination in the United Church of Canada while Lincoln, embracing the social revolution of the 1960s, smoked pot, grew his hair long, and took part in campus protests. His mother recognized the back of his head in a front-page photo in the *Vancouver Sun*, taken when Jerry Rubin, the American anti-war activist, and his pet pig led a group of UBC students in an occupation of the university's faculty club.

"How did she handle that?" I ask him when I first hear the story, almost a decade later.

"She was mad at me," he says. "And I made her cry. I hated that I made her cry."

Lincoln has been driving back and forth between Grand Forks and Abbotsford, tending to house and garden and supporting Naomi, who is home for the summer, working and worrying about her grandmother. He is, thankfully, in Abbotsford with his mom and me when I leave her side to shake him awake early one morning and tell him that her pulse is thready, her breaths very far apart. By the time we are with her, just seconds later, she has left us. It is the first time I see my husband cry. He cries again when he tells his dad and his sister, both of them in long-term care. His father lives with advanced dementia, and Christine with late-stage Parkinson's disease.

His whole family! How does he bear it?

We complete the paperwork, empty the apartment, scrub it clean, and have it repainted. Essie would approve, I think. We make one last visit to Jimmy before heading home to Grand Forks.

"We'll be back to see you in two weeks," we tell him.

It has been a long time since we've had any idea of what he understands. We make sure the staff know our plans. We mark the date for our return on Christine's calendar.

"I can't believe she's gone," she says.

We leave the Fraser Valley the next morning and head for home. Between Chilliwack and Hope we drive through a series of sun showers, small, glorious islands of rain that fall from isolated clouds while the sun shines in the in-between patches of blue. Rainbow after rainbow blooms in the sky. We both feel it—a welcome-home celebration for this little, lovely woman who believed in a loving God and all his angels.

"See, Chookie," I can hear her saying. "How can you look at that and not believe?"

We arrive home exhausted and relieved. We need rest and walks and a chance to breathe. The light is flashing on the answering machine. I am tempted to leave it until the morning.

"It's probably my mom," I tell Lincoln as I pick up the phone. "I'd better check it."

It isn't my mom. It's the Menno Home in Abbotsford. Lincoln's father is dead.

In the new year, after Christmas with our girls, Lincoln and I load up our vw camper with a plan to head south to the Mexican sun. We are battered by loss but so grateful we are not working. Grief teaches us a new gentleness with each other—being wounded, we are careful not to wound.

First, we drive to Abbotsford to say goodbye to Christine, and then we take the ferry to Victoria to see my parents and our girls. My mother lives independently and my father, wheelchair bound and disappearing into late-stage Alzheimer's, is in a long-term care home.

Just days later, we are slowly driving the length of the Baja peninsula, poking our way through small villages, every one preceded by a sign—TOPES—that warns of the speed bumps ahead. We dodge potholes, washouts, and the occasional cow, always on the lookout for the perfect place to stop for a meal or to spend the night. We are never far from the sea, and we drive with our windows down to catch the breeze and the ocean's hush. We have no plan other than to be guided by the impulse of the moment, staying as long as we want in one place, moving on according to some criterion that is never spoken but on which we seem to agree. Evenings, we toast the setting sun with Mexican beer while watching the pelican glide-and-dive show, and we pass the time before bed with games of backgammon. Often I read aloud, a habit we've picked up over years of camping together. No deep philosophy for our simple brains. *Harry Potter and the Philosopher's Stone* is our book of choice.

After two idyllic months, I feel anxieties rising. Lincoln and I have escaped the worst of the winter and there is an easing in the intensity of our sadness, but I need to see our girls and Lincoln's sister. They haven't had this lovely respite and I don't know how they are bearing up under their burdens of grief. I need to see my parents. It's time to go home.

The border crossing between Tijuana and San Diego is a chaos of colour and honking horns, street stalls, wandering vendors, and tiny children, with even tinier children tied to their backs, silently begging from car to car. We give away the last of our pesos, and it's a guilt-ridden relief to be finally through the border, to be away from those sad eyes. But how can anyone really leave them behind?

We have been out of email contact for the last couple of days as we pushed our way north and neither of us owns a cellphone. Once in the States, we pull into the first freeway rest area so I can call my mother from a pay phone and let her know we are on our way home. My older sister, Margaret, answers the phone.

"Oh, honey," she says.

"What is it?" I ask, though I know. I hear it in her voice. I know.

"Dad died three days ago."

While I sob in the rest area on the freeway, Lincoln makes a plan. I will fly home from Los Angeles. He will drive the van and meet me in Victoria. The trip takes him three days of almost non-stop driving. All I can think as I make my way to my mother's side is that I can't imagine my mom without my dad. Even though he's been sick for almost six years, even though he has utterly changed, I can't imagine her without him.

I am still in Victoria, just weeks after my father's death, when my uncle dies in Saskatchewan. Within months, there is another call from the Menno Home in Abbotsford. Christine is dying. We are still an hour away when she takes her last breath.

"She died alone," Lincoln says. "No one should have to die alone."

"No," I say. And then I ask what we have been asking each other, over and over, since Essie's death.

"What do you need? How can I help?"

"I need this to be over," he says.

It must be over, I think. *Who is left to die?*

The lessons of profound loss are simple: Life is short. Joy is fleeting. And so, in the spring of 2005, Lincoln plans a summer adventure. Because he is eight and a half years older than I am, he retires when I still have a few years left to work. Hutton School in Grand Forks, British Columbia, is going to miss its well-loved teacher-librarian, and he will miss the kids, his colleagues, and his beautiful library. And I will miss him. I don't mind that he is going but I will miss him. His retirement gift from me, one that he chooses himself, is a Bike Friday, an ingenious folding bicycle he will pedal from Paris to Istanbul, following the Orient Express route. I am grateful he will be part of a small tour group for he is, at best, a terrible correspondent and not comfortable or proficient with email. Before he leaves, I slip a note into his backpack that reads: *Just in case you have too much fun, remember to whom you belong. Come home to me.* I include a poem I wrote for him.

I Am Bound

I am bound to my man of the hills
And he is bound to me
We lump and bump over stone and stump
Crag and meadow alike to greet
Startle the marmot on his whistling rock
I cling to moss, he scales a peak
But we are tethered to we.

I wander alongside my travelling man
And he wanders along beside me
A winding road, sirens' lament
Valleys, vistas, and Berber tents
Cedar and cactus, the moon's eclipse
To a slip of a child with a wink of a smile
We speak with our hands, a nod, a grin
He wants to keep roaming
I want to be homing
He wanders along with me.

I share a canoe with old river man
And he shares a canoe with me
Whitewater foam becomes his home
Tranquil shore with sand for my toes
Onward he paddles
While backwards I dig
That moose in the lilies is much too big!
But we share our boat
We stay afloat
Old river man and me.

We make a home in the heart of a town
In mountain's shadow, by river's edge
We lose our days in children's play
Hills are tamed by small ones' steps
Rivers calmed by small ones' fears
Our hearts near burst to watch them grow
I hold them close, he helps them go
We play our part, love harbours we
My gentle man and me.

He calls me from Paris when he finds the poem. He tells me that it brought tears to his eyes.

"Oh, sweetheart," I say. "I didn't mean to make you cry." Secretly, I am thrilled.

Less than a year later, in January 2006, Lincoln empties the big glass jar that sits on top of our fridge of its accumulation of loonies and toonies. We've been adding to it for over a decade. There is a picture of an iconic mountain taped to the outside and a label: The Kilimanjar Jar. Lincoln is about to realize a dream. He will fly to Tanzania to join an expedition to climb Mount Kilimanjaro. Just months earlier he completed the bike trip from Paris to Istanbul, and I have confidence in his abilities and resilience. He returns from Africa with a souvenir T-shirt, a few cans of Kilimanjaro beer for his friends, and something else—something that comes very close to killing him.

Though Lincoln struggled during the final push to the summit, he put his difficulties down to altitude sickness. He knew he was in serious trouble after the descent. The other climbers who experienced symptoms of altitude sickness all felt better once they returned to lower ground, but Lincoln never did. He struggled to breathe for

the whole next week while touring the Ngorongoro Crater.

Then he pushed himself from Africa to Amsterdam, Amsterdam to London, London to Vancouver, and finally Vancouver to Kelowna. He picked up the car in the long-term parking lot at the Kelowna airport and made the bizarre decision to take it through a car wash before driving himself home. Kelowna is a three-hour drive from our home in Grand Forks. It is early evening when he pulls into our carport, and even under the pale outdoor lights, I can see how sick he is, how grey.

"You're not okay," I say.

"No. I'm not."

"Get back in the car. We're going to the hospital."

He shakes his head and then he starts to cry. He never admits to feeling unwell. He rarely cries.

"Just let me come in and sit down, Les. Just let me have a cup of tea."

I give him tea but he won't eat anything. His breathing is shallow and rapid and he frequently gulps for air, like a fish out of water.

He has asthma but exercise has never been a trigger. And this does not look like any asthma attack I have ever witnessed. It takes me hours to bully him back into the car. I reason. I beg. I stomp and rage. I sob while threatening to call an ambulance. I don't know why I don't. He can talk. He can walk. I guess that's why. Finally, he agrees to go if I let him unpack.

The nurses in the emergency room give him oxygen and ask him questions. His story changes with every conversation. At one point he is chatty, almost giddy.

"He's not himself," I tell the nurses. "He's acting strangely. He never talks like that."

"He's happy to see you!" someone says.

They don't want to wake up the doctor on call because Lincoln is so damn cheerful, though his breathing is compromised. One of the nurses checks his feet and legs repeatedly. She asks if he experienced any pain on the flight home or after.

"No," he says.

When the doctor arrives, Lincoln tells yet another version of his story before disappearing to the X-ray department. Soon the doctor shows me the X-ray film and draws a circle with his finger around a shadow in the bottom of one lung.

"Pneumonia," he tells me. "Or pleurisy. We can start him on antibiotics and you can probably take him home."

"I'm not taking him home until he is breathing comfortably and his colour improves," I say. "Please. He isn't making any sense. He's telling everyone a different story."

At this point, our family doctor shows up. He knows Lincoln well. They are kayaking and mountain biking buddies.

"You look like hell," he tells him.

"I feel like hell," Lincoln says.

Our doctor checks the X-ray and orders a blood test, one that will directly measure the amount of oxygen in his blood. The lab tech is back quickly with the results. He and the doctor try to keep their faces professionally neutral, but there is tension and concern in the quick looks they flash at Lincoln and at me.

"I'm sending him to Kelowna right now," our doctor tells me as he walks toward us. "You go home and grab a toothbrush. You can follow the ambulance."

"Can't I ride with him?"

"No."

The rest is a blur. Did I say goodbye to him? I must have. My foot bounces on the gas pedal as I drive home. I panic when I realize I don't know where the hospital is in Kelowna. I struggle with a wayfinding application on my new computer and give up in frustration. I call close friends, Liz and Jean, because Liz has just had knee surgery in Kelowna. She'll be able to give me directions. Jean is soon at my door; she will drive me to Kelowna. She is calm and cheerful and has already arranged for us to spend the night with mutual friends there.

In the Kelowna hospital, a very kind respirologist meets with us in the crowded, chaotic emergency department. He tells me it isn't pneumonia but a blood clot in his lung. A pulmonary embolism.

I've read about those. They can develop in healthy people who sit in one position for too long, like on a plane from Canada to East Africa. Typically they start in a leg and cause considerable pain. That's why that smart nurse kept asking him about his legs. They can be painless, however, and start in the groin or the belly. They kill people. Untreated, the mortality rate can be as high as thirty percent.

"It's been there a while," the specialist says, "judging from the amount of fluid that has gathered around it."

He explains how it will be treated—"big gun" drugs to bust it up, then a maintenance dose of warfarin, frequent blood tests for monitoring, and a follow-up scan to make sure there are no other clots lurking in his body.

"He's had a close call," he says. "He should be fine. Good thing he's so fit."

He theorizes that Lincoln developed the clot on the plane trip to Africa and popped it into his lung during the ascent of the mountain. What Lincoln thought were the effects of altitude sickness was the embolism messing with his breathing capacity. We practise the new vocabulary. Pulmonary embolism. PE for short. We also learn that this "close call" is a bit of a miracle. In his report, the specialist describes him as a fit older gentleman. He also says he is delightful and stoic.

"Only you could be so reckless and come away smelling like a rose!" I tell Lincoln. "Why didn't you go to a hospital in Tanzania? You could have died."

"I was sure I was going to die," he says. "I figured if I could stay alive until I was on the plane to Amsterdam, or maybe even London, that would be easier for you. I didn't think I was coming home, Les."

What could I say? So many times in our life together, I have wanted to strangle him. And so many times he has slipped the noose with that stoicism, that sweet charm. And he came home. If he had done the sensible thing and sought medical help in Tanzania, would they have picked up on the embolism or would they have treated him for pneumonia? Would he have come home? What could I say?

After a couple of days in the Kelowna hospital, he is transferred back to an acute care room in Grand Forks. The few visitors I permit all comment first on how lucky he is and then on how blue his lips are. He looks and feels so much better that the blue lips don't bother me. When his colour fully returns, he is discharged with medication and ordered to take it easy until further tests assure us he is free of blood clots, and the doses of blood thinners can be reduced.

When he fully recovers, and he does, ahead of schedule, we blithely joke about it. We call it "an almost-kick-the-bucket trip." I rename the mountain "Kill-my-man-jaro."

The night terrors start shortly after his return. They are violent, active dreams in which he shouts and thrashes about, sometimes even leaping out of bed. They occur a couple of times a month, and I question our doctor about the possibility of a connection to the embolism. He doesn't think there is a relationship and suggests that maybe they are a quiet guy's way of working through a stressful time, possibly a mild form of post-traumatic stress disorder.

At the time, we are far more grateful that Lincoln has made his way home than we are concerned about a few weird dreams.

2 *Slipping Sideways*

IT BEGINS WITH THOSE NIGHT TERRORS. Over the next few years they gradually increase in frequency and intensity, though in the daytime he seems normal and untroubled. But at night he startles awake, shouts, flings off the bedding, searches frantically for small animals among the tangle of sheets, or begs me to run with him from dogs and men with axes. I fumble for the lamp switch and beg him to wake up, to open his eyes. I hold him and tell him over and over that he's okay.

I buy a lamp for my bedside table that I can control with a clap of my hands. I think I will be able to get the room lit quickly and spare him a few seconds of that dreadful panic.

One night I am jolted out of sleep by a frenzied tugging of the sheets.

"Get out! Get out!" Lincoln shouts.

"Honey!" I cry. "It's okay!"

Then I bang my hands together with as much force as I can muster, a single, sharp, loud smack that not only fails to turn on the lamp but startles Lincoln and sends him stumbling away from me, tripping over the duvet on the floor, careening off furniture, and still shouting "Get out!" while I clap like a madwoman—and the lamp never does turn on.

I fly out of bed to slap at the wall switch for the overhead light. Lincoln and I are both caught, frozen in that sudden flash of brightness, like escaping prisoners trapped in a searchlight's beam in an old movie. All that is missing is the wail of sirens. We look at each other and fumble our way together. We don't hug; we cling. I feel his heart thumping against my chest and I am sure he can feel mine. I settle him back into the bed, and as I tuck the sheets around him, I explain about the lamp and apologize for the clapping.

"Is that what that was?" he asks and starts to laugh. "I thought someone was shooting at us!"

Over the five years after Lincoln's return from Kilimanjaro, until the spring of 2011, our lives evolve much as we anticipated. In August 2006, we walk for two weeks across rural England, from the Irish Sea to the North Sea on the Coast to Coast path. For me, it is a walk through the movie sets of literature that I love, in the footsteps of the romantic poets, the Brontës, James Herriot, and A.A. Milne. Lincoln's cousin and her husband join us for a few days, and after we finish walking, we have time to visit them at home in Derbyshire. Derbyshire! Jane Austen! Elizabeth Bennet! Mr. Darcy and Pemberley! More of Lincoln's delightful English relatives welcome us. It is good for us both to reconnect with those who also loved Essie, Jim, and Christine—to share tears and memories—and it is especially healing for Lincoln. Other than our girls and me, he has no family in Canada.

In the summer of 2008, I join Lincoln in retirement, a retirement in which we fulfill the promises made when we were young, promises to always allow adventure into our lives and to never hold each other back. Together, we hike our valley's trails and mountain paths in BC and Alberta. When we aren't travelling, our winter days are filled with snowshoe and cross-country ski trips and our summers with camping, kayaking, or canoeing. We pick up the travelling life we willingly abandoned thirty years before, a life exchanged for the privilege of living, teaching, and raising our two children in a beautiful little town.

We are circling back to our early days, our travelling days, and we delight in the freedom. Several winters in a row, we wander the familiar route to the southern tip of the Baja peninsula and up its windswept eastern cape. We free-camp in palm-sheltered bays, paddling our kayak to the sound of dolphin breath and the cranky barking of seal colonies.

We rock in a small panga while grey whale mommas and their babies slip and roll around us. We putter up and down the west coast of Canada and the United States, clambering down cliffsides to reach hidden beaches, wandering among giant redwoods, cedars, and Douglas firs. We hike the slick rock canyons of Colorado and Utah. In Joshua Tree National Park we dig through our orange crate of CDs for the U2 album of the same name and quietly play it on our old ghetto blaster as the setting sun bleeds crimson and gold into the Sonoran Desert sky.

The mountain-ringed lakes of British Columbia's backcountry call us home. I have only to catch the faintest whiff of woodsmoke to be transported to the glow of flickering campfires and deep contentment. We love each other most easily when we are on the road and we talk often about gratitude. I don't think there is a moment during which we do not have a sense of our privilege, our enormous good fortune in having each other, our girls well and happy, Sarah in Ontario working on a master's degree in cultural anthropology and Naomi completing her teaching degree at the University of Victoria.

When Naomi accepts a teaching contract in Lax Kw'alaams, on the north coast of BC, we take it as an invitation to explore northern rainforests where eagles fill the sky in numbers too large to count. We fall in love with the north and make plans to return and carry on to the Yukon and Alaska.

And then life slips sideways.

Aside from the night terrors, Lincoln seems much as he has always been—perhaps a little more indecisive, a little more dependent on me for company, but I must confess that I like that. It is not always easy to be the spouse of a man determined to follow his own path in all things. We have experienced huge challenges in our relationship but neither of us can tolerate unhappiness for any length of time, so we take turns pushing each other toward resolution of our differences. He loves me enough to seek help when I ask, even when he thinks it unnecessary. And I love him enough to shut up and listen, to give a quiet soul room to breathe and time to think. And we practise forgiveness. We worry together about our kids and delight in their well-being. We hold each other up through all those close-together deaths—his parents, his sister, my dad, and my mother's youngest brother. That time, intense and grief burdened as it was, reveals the deeper measure of our love for each other. We are each other's best comfort. We look at the world in similar ways. We share the same values. And we make each other laugh. We are good friends.

I enjoy finding him more often by my side and needing me . . . just a little bit. When I notice him quiet and withdrawn on social occasions, I dismiss it as problems with his hearing. He has been profoundly deaf in one ear since childhood and he is in his late sixties, fit and strong, but not a young man. He has never had any patience with small talk or schmoozing.

The first time he struggles with the income taxes, I am relieved to have it all packed up and delivered to an accountant instead of littering the dining room table.

"We've worked hard all our lives, sweetheart," I say. "Let someone else handle this. Wouldn't you rather go for a hike?"

His uncanny sense of direction seems to be deserting him but mine has always been so dreadful that no alarm bells ring, or if they do, I refuse to listen. I cover my ears with my hands and tell myself what I need to hear.

"He's okay," I repeat to myself. "He's getting older. That's all. He's okay."

Naomi and her partner, Isaac, are spending a year in Costa Rica at Isaac's family's farm. I find myself making all the plans for a trip to visit them and tour the national parks with a small adventure company. Lincoln happily goes along with all my decisions.

Great, I think. *That was easy!*

I do not acknowledge that it is completely out of character for him to be so compliant. Close friends tentatively express concerns and ask questions I can't or won't answer.

"Is Lincoln okay?" they say.

They tell me stories about how confused he seems when they are making plans, how he sometimes asks the same questions over and over. We buy a new car and he cannot figure it out. Little things, like the window buttons, door locks, and mirror positions, and the big things—backing up, parking between the lines—they all confound him.

"He's getting old," I insist in defensive explanation of his behaviour. "He's driven the same vehicle for fifteen years!"

Denial is a wonderful thing. Until it isn't.

———

The day before we leave for Costa Rica, I experience an uncontrollable tremor in my left arm as I am putting on my coat, a tremor that persists and increases in frequency throughout the month we are in Central America.

It's a pinched nerve, I tell myself. *Something to do with my shoulder injury.*

That's not all. I have been seeing a physiotherapist about severe pain in my right shoulder and mention to him that occasionally

I feel as if my left leg is unresponsive, that I must consciously focus on it to get it moving properly. He watches me walk and sees nothing unusual in my gait.

"It looks good," he tells me, "but if it persists, come back and I'll do a thorough neuro workup."

I cling to "looks good" and put "neuro workup" out of my mind.

It isn't until we are in Costa Rica, that February of 2011, and I am unable to keep my flip-flop sandal on my left foot, that I allow myself to begin to consider that something more serious than a pinched nerve might be wrong with me. I test my left foot and hand, my left arm and leg. I can trigger the tremor by holding my arm out straight or doing up a zipper. My leg drags to the point of tripping me up if am tired and forget to make it "walk properly." If I stand on tiptoe, my left heel sinks immediately to the ground. If I stand on my heels, my right-foot toes remain up, pointing skyward, while the left ones drop quickly.

Lincoln takes a zip-lining excursion through the Costa Rican jungle, but I am now on a waiting list for shoulder surgery and choose a rainforest canopy walk as a safer option. When we meet up after our separate adventures, he is upset.

"I couldn't figure it out," he tells me. "I had to go tandem with one of the guides!"

I am, at first, shocked and dismayed. He is a rock climber, used to ropes and unafraid of heights, and has always been physically coordinated and quick to learn, with extraordinary stamina and balance. Then I begin to rationalize his experience.

"You're left-handed," I remind him. "And you don't speak any Spanish. And you're deaf in one ear. Anyone would find it tricky!"

What does my cheerfulness cost him? Does it hurt? Is it reassuring? I don't know. I wonder if my unwillingness to see his struggles is the result of my fears about my own health.

Between us we have an accumulation of changes, many small, some large, but we are both still very much ourselves, content with each other and the good fortune of our lives, getting older but not yet old. It is easier to pretend all is well in our world because, really, it is. Some of the time. Enough of the time.

———————

As soon as we are home from Costa Rica, I call our doctor's office to make an appointment. Our family physician is out of town but I am able to meet with his locum that same day. I am pleased to hear I will be seeing the mother of a former student, an empathetic, holistic practitioner. I know she will listen to my concerns. Lincoln comes with me, and at the end of our visit, the doctor asks us to return later that same day, after the clinic's official closing time.

"I'd like to spend more time with you," she says. "This seems neurological. I need to make some calls."

When we return, she tells us she has contacted a neurologist in Kelowna who has agreed to see me within three months. My shoulder surgery will have to be postponed until neurological issues, if any, have been identified. Multiple sclerosis is unlikely at my age; it is usually diagnosed in younger people. Parkinson's is a possibility, though I am a little younger than the typical age of onset. She suggests I start taking a high-quality fish oil. Essential fatty acids are good for the brain. She encourages me to understand that this could be many things—some benign and, yes, some scary.

"I know it's hard, but try not to worry," she says.

For the next three months I ride waves of positive thinking—when I am not drowning in worst-case scenarios. I wake in the middle of the night and search the internet for clues to what is wrong with me. I find myself hoping for a benign brain tumour instead of one of the diseases that seem to match my symptoms. They all have abbreviations—ALS, PD, MSA, PSP—and frightening actual names: amyotrophic lateral sclerosis, Parkinson's disease, multiple system atrophy, progressive supranuclear palsy. Every one of them is progressive and none of them is curable.

It seems a very long three months but everyone else I know in British Columbia who has needed a referral to a neurologist has waited a year or more. What must that feel like?

Now the dilemma is: Who do we tell and when do we tell them? Sarah and Naomi are aware of the situation but I haven't said anything to my mother or my siblings.

Families are like small ecosystems, interdependent, sustaining, and constantly adjusting to external pressures. I am proud of the way ours functions, the way we have recovered from misunderstandings and periods of estrangement. I am proud that we are close, that despite our strong and very different personalities, my siblings and I are united in our concern for our mom and for one another. Every one of us has a big life, with multiple responsibilities and challenges. I hate to disrupt our ecosystem, to add stress to the load everyone is already carrying, but how can I continue to keep my anxiety about my health from these people I love so much?

My mom, still living independently in Victoria, is deeply grieving my father's death and exhibiting symptoms of vascular dementia, especially short-term memory loss. She is bright as can be in the moment but the moments are repeating themselves with alarming frequency. My older sister, Margaret, lives in Vancouver; my younger sister, Jane, on the Sunshine Coast. Because my older brother, Bill, is the only one of us living in Victoria, he is our mother's main support.

I write:

Dear Family,

This is not news to Naomi and Sarah and I have struggled with the "should I or should I not" of involving everyone at this point. But if it were one of you, I would want to know, so here I go.

In a long email I tell them about my wayward left foot, my wooden left leg, and the tremor. I think they will be reassured that I have a referral in the works and I know they understand how supportive Lincoln is.

"No freaking out," I tell them. "This is a wobble, not a blow."

I am alone in the basement waiting area of an unfamiliar hospital. Lincoln waits for me in another ugly room of vinyl chairs and old magazines. Our family doctor has ordered a CT scan of my brain. He wonders if I've had a stroke. It seems a good idea to at least start ruling things out while I wait to see the neurologist. I don't like small spaces. I am nervous about the scan, and the anxiety pushes my tremor into overdrive.

The technician is abrupt. She questions me about any metal I might be wearing or any surgical implants. She stresses the importance of not moving. It isn't a long procedure but it's long enough for her to bark at me twice to lie still. I've been told not to talk, so I don't respond. In a weird way, her lack of sensitivity helps. Everyone around me has responded to my situation with such kindness and concern. I appreciate the sympathy but I don't like being that person, the one about whom others worry. This woman is clearly not sympathetic and maybe I don't want her to be. I am taking indignant pleasure in her lack of empathy.

Not okay, I think. Both her and whatever is wrong me. *Not okay*.

While the machine hums and clicks, I spend the rest of the time wondering why she is so grumpy and feeling a little sorry for her. I mentally practise how I will tell the story to Lincoln. It's good to have the chance to hone my delivery. It's a good distraction.

"How did it go?" he asks, as I walk back into the waiting room.

"She wasn't very nice. She kept telling me to lie still."

"Did you tell her . . . ?"

"I wasn't supposed to talk so I didn't say anything. I just yelled at her inside my head."

It feels good to say it out loud and I laugh as I deliver the punchline. Lincoln laughs, too. The irony is not lost on him.

"Lady," I say, "I have a tremor. If I could lie still, I wouldn't be here!"

I don't want Lincoln to come in to see the neurologist with me; I insist he remain in the waiting room. It's his birthday. My husband is turning sixty-eight years old and I am sure I have Parkinson's disease. Nothing showed up on the scan—Parkinson's doesn't— and my symptoms have become increasingly consistent with the descriptions I find online. I think I will better handle the news if I don't have to witness his reaction. We know enough, after Christine's painful and premature death, to be frightened of what a future with Parkinson's may hold. And there is our shared concern about what might be going on with him, a concern temporarily displaced by our worries about me.

I find the neurologist courteous and professional. He spends thirty minutes tapping and testing my reflexes. He asks me to stand and gives my shoulders a quick tug. He has to catch me before I fall over. I push against his hands and he pushes back. He gets me to do lots of kindergarten-style hand actions, which I should be really good at but am not, and watches me walk in all kinds of ways and try to balance, sometimes not very well.

He tells me it's Parkinson's. There is no need for medication, not yet. I am to keep as active as I can. My shoulder surgery can go ahead. An MRI is not necessary as it is definitely not multiple sclerosis. I tell him I am not surprised and my eyes fill with tears.

I walk out of the examination area and into the waiting room. I speak briefly with the receptionist and schedule a follow-up appointment for six months down the road. I smile at Lincoln.

"I'll tell you in the car," I whisper.

We ride the elevator down in silence. We walk to the car the same way.

I climb into the front passenger seat, close the door, and turn to look at my husband.

"It's Parkinson's," I say. "The doctor says there's nothing else it could be."

I don't know what he says in response. Or if he says anything at all. I sob for a long time while he holds me. And then we head for home. Maybe fifteen minutes later, maybe half an hour, we find ourselves high in the hills above Kelowna on an unfamiliar, winding rural road.

"Hey, babe," I say, finally able to take in our surroundings. "Where are we?"

After a long moment he answers.

"I've no idea," he says.

I am thankful to have visited Naomi and Isaac in Costa Rica. It was a chance to get to know the easygoing, creative young man who has our daughter's heart. Isaac spent several years of his childhood on the farm, a mountainside, rainforest paradise that was once a coffee plantation. His family has purposefully worked on rewilding the jungle that surrounds the house and guest cabin. Isaac is a fluent speaker of Spanish and through him we were able to talk with friends and neighbours. He and Naomi mucked about in their newly planted vegetable garden and gathered eggs from their chickens. I was enchanted by the orchids winding their way along tree trunks and the macaws and monkeys that chattered and squawked from the canopy. One day, Isaac drove the farm truck down the mountain to an isolated coastal beach, and almost every day, we walked the jungle path to the waterfall and swimming hole on the property.

I hate the thought of my health woes intruding on Naomi's time in this magical place, but I make the phone call. Though she has seen the tremor and my misbehaving left foot, she is still dismayed by the news.

"I'm coming home, Mom," she says.

I am ready for this—I know her empathetic heart—and have my arguments in place. I tell her I am fine, there is nothing to be done but to learn to live with the diagnosis, and that is work I must do on my own. I tell her I know she loves us both very much. I tell her how happy her father and I are that she and Isaac are enjoying this year together and how distressed we would be if she cut her stay short because of my Parkinson's. Everything I say is true. I am quickly learning the disease touches more lives than just my own. The grief is shared with those I love, and somehow that makes the weight of bearing it both heavier and lighter at the same time.

"Please don't come home, honey," I beg. "We can talk every day."

She reluctantly agrees after eliciting a promise from me to tell her if things get worse.

Sarah, our anthropologist child, has completely altered her career path. Halfway through her master's degree she realized that academia was not the place for her. She did not want to teach, and "publish or perish" held no appeal.

"I'm starting an apprenticeship," she told us. "I'm going to be an electrician."

"If that works for you, it works for us," we said.

She and her husband, Jason, also an electrician, met on the job in Victoria. They both worked at Mica Dam, renovating an old house in Revelstoke on their days off.

Nine years later, I ask her if she remembers the moment I told her the neurologist had confirmed my suspicion that I had Parkinson's.

"I'm sorry, Mom," she says. "I don't remember. That sounds awful . . . but I don't."

"Don't apologize, sweetheart," I say. "I can't remember either. That's why I am asking. I know I must have told you but there's no email . . ."

"There wouldn't be," she explains. "We were living in the old camp with no Wi-Fi and no cell service. I could only have called you on the pay phone."

We agree on all the main points—that she knew there was something wrong, what my symptoms were, and that I suspected Parkinson's. We laugh a little at the shared hole in our memories.

"What I remember from that time is your shoulder pain and how awful it was," she says. "I think I was way more worried about that and hoping you would get surgery soon."

As she speaks I remember those pain-filled days, how every movement hurt, how I couldn't lie down and spent long nights in the recliner, how the doctor finally prescribed morphine so I could sleep.

Is it strange that the story I am now telling myself about those days gives such little space to the physical pain I was experiencing and so much to the emotional? Is it perhaps because the shoulder-pain story ends happily?

My siblings are very aware of my shoulder issue and now I have this diagnosis to share with them. I hate being the bad-news sister but I can't put it off any longer. I choose email so I can present the most positive version of events without the blubbering that would surely punctuate any phone calls. It feels good to hit the bottom of the rabbit hole, to know what I am dealing with. Now the challenge is to figure out how to live in this altered universe.

I ask my brother to tell Mom for me.

"You can tell her I'm fine," I say, "but I won't be able to talk yet without blubbering. I'll give it a few days. She knows me. She'll understand."

"Of course," Bill says. "I'll tell her . . . but one question. Am I allowed to blubber?"

My father met my mother just before he enlisted in the army and disappeared to Europe for almost five years. In his absence, my mother completed a nursing degree at the University of Saskatchewan in Saskatoon and went to work caring for wounded soldiers at Shaughnessy Hospital in Vancouver. My father landed in Normandy as part of the D-Day invasion forces and fought his way across France and Holland and into Germany. He was a man who loved to talk but he had little to say about the war. When asked about Normandy, his stock answer was, "I got my feet wet." He had a Mention in Dispatches tacked up on the wall in his study.

"What's this for, Dad?" we'd ask him.

"For brushing my teeth."

Two weeks after his return to Canada, he married my mother. They lived in Saskatoon while Dad completed his bachelor of divinity degree. Fast-forward through a return to military life, the birth of four army brats in nine years, multiple moves through four provinces, and a return to civilian life, and my dad was now a compassionate pastor, a respected scholar, and a successful freelance writer.

He could be cranky and impatient, and we never cut him an inch of slack for whatever the war might have done to the bright, sensitive young man who "got his feet wet" on a Normandy beach. The ghosts of war appeared with a vengeance and plagued his sleep when he developed Alzheimer's.

I think often of my father as we come to terms with my diagnosis and find ourselves unable to deny that Lincoln is struggling with cognitive issues. We know dementia, know it too well. Both our fathers died of Alzheimer's. I thought that taught us how to bear heartbreak.

"I want to go home," my father would say.

"Dad, you're home," I told him. "You're home."

But the familiar room with its books, including the two he had written, the paintings he and my mother collected over their sixty years together, and the family photos was no longer a haven of peace and comfort. I thought at the time that it was just his inability to connect to the externals of his environment that so disoriented him.

And Jimmy, Lincoln's dad, would pore over tiny photographs mounted in leather-bound booklets tied with fraying laces. These moments, from a life almost seventy years gone, before the war, before Canada, before kids, seemed to hold more meaning than his wife, his son and daughter, or our two girls, his only grandchildren and the light of his life no longer. He would point to a sepia street scene, brick row houses with front steps leading down to cobblestones, and he would whisper to himself in his soft Lancashire accent, "Openshaw." It was the district in Manchester where he grew up and lived until he emigrated to Canada with his young family after the war. He could not have told you his own name.

I wonder now if our fathers were trying to tell us not so much that they couldn't make sense of what they were seeing, but that they could no longer make sense of what they were feeling, their internal landscapes having become as unfamiliar as the external ones. They must have needed something to cling to, something that meant, "It's okay. I know this. I'm home."

Our nights are increasingly interrupted by Lincoln's nightmares and our days troubled by his confusion. I urge him to go to the doctor but he resists. I understand his reluctance. It is unbearable to think that we are once again confronting this horror. It is a long, hard journey, and I cannot imagine having the strength to handle losing Lincoln in such a cruel way. Our fathers presented with symptoms in their eighties. Lincoln is not yet seventy. And I fear his reaction even more. How will my free-spirited, outdoor-loving, adrenalin-fuelled man adapt to the constraints, to the disease's determination to take everything he loves from him? I am angry that this could be his, our, future. I anticipate his anger and frustration or worse, deep depression, and brace myself for what might come. We talk about it and he is open and matter of fact, surprisingly positive.

"One day at a time," he says.

I ask him again to go to the doctor. And, again, he tells me he doesn't want to.

"What can he do for me, Les?" he says.

"We can't know until we ask."

Finally, he goes. We go together. Lincoln does not perform well on the cognitive screening test. He can't draw a cube or a clock or remember the list of words or count backwards by sevens. Our doctor is surprised but I am not.

"Probably Alzheimer's," he tells us and he prescribes medication. Aricept. I've seen the ads. Happy, grey-haired couples living the Alzheimer's good life. They could as easily have been in an ad for a cruise line. Nowhere in the faces of the smiling models do I see the dimming of the light, the bewilderment in the eyes I am so familiar with, which I imagine I see beginning to reveal itself in Lincoln's eyes, even at this early stage. Lincoln tries. He tries so hard. The pills leave him depressed for the first time in his life and they make him physically ill. And no one can assure us that they will make one bit of difference in the end. After a month's trial, he stops taking them, and I cannot bring myself to add to his misery by arguing that he continue.

We make the choice to be as open about Lincoln's illness as we have been about mine, to not close ourselves off or pretend all is right in our world. I understand it will be hard news for people to hear. And we are, along with almost everyone we know, mourning the recent loss of a beloved friend—David—one of a small group of outdoor-loving men, including Lincoln, we call the Lost Boys. There is lately, for me, such poignant irony in the name.

That openness is the best decision we can make. We continue to be included in social gatherings; we even make new friends. Three good men offer to take Lincoln on what will be his last canoe trip, ten days away from home on beautiful Murtle Lake in Wells Gray Provincial Park. He is overjoyed at being included but worried about doing it without me. And so am I.

"You must sleep in the same tent with him," I tell our friend John, who has agreed to partner Lincoln in the canoe.

You go with him if he goes out of the tent to pee.

You go to the outhouse with him.

You know he has night terrors.

He doesn't always dress according to the weather.

He's not as strong as he used to be, not nearly as strong.

Thank you, thank you, thank you.

Lincoln starts packing weeks in advance. When I am unable to convince him of the "less is more" policy of canoe-tripping, I invite John over to help us winnow the piles of clothing and gear. As I listen to John's good-humoured, patient guidance, I am forced to confront my own impatience.

That's how it's done, I tell myself.

While Lincoln is away, I have the second of my two shoulder surgeries. I managed to shred my rotator cuffs as a novice paddler with our local dragon boat team. The pain at times has been overwhelming, but the first surgery went well and I am looking forward to similar relief following this next one. Between us, we rely on the support of at least a dozen friends during the week and a half of his absence and my surgery. Our next-door neighbour drives me over the pass to the hospital in Trail two days in a row when my surgery is cancelled on the first day. Another friend insists that I am brought from the hospital to her house so she can look after me while the anaesthetic wears off, I figure out the pain management, and get my Parkinson's medications back on track. Others bring meals and books and encourage me to get out for walks, ready to catch me if I stumble.

I don't take it for granted and am overwhelmed by the remarkable kindness that sustains us for days and weeks and months that become years.

My mind has always behaved chaotically. Lincoln and I used to laugh at the non sequiturs that peppered my conversations when a piece of my thoughts would fall out of my mouth with no expressed context for the listener.

"I have no idea what you're talking about," he would say. "Sometimes you scare me!"

We are in the car, running errands. Lincoln is driving and unable to figure out how to get into the credit union parking lot, despite my directions. We circle the block a few times before I suggest we just go home.

"Sometimes you scare me," I say when we are parked in our driveway.

I regret the words, hate them and myself, the minute they are out of my mouth. I wanted to ease the tension that radiated from him. To make a joke. It's a stupid thing I do sometimes when I'm stressed.

"I scare myself," he says quietly.

And then he starts to chuckle. I love him so much in this moment, for the kindness of his beautiful sense of humour. The forgiveness it contains. And for all that comes after, for all the sorrow and the pain, we have that. It is no small thing.

We decide it's time for Lincoln to grant me power of attorney. I am grateful that he is so amenable to the process. I meet once with the notary in order to describe our circumstances, and she is empathetic but very clear.

"This needs to be done now," she explains, "while Lincoln can still demonstrate enough mental competency to prove he understands the implications of the decision."

She tells me that I can be present while she speaks with him but I cannot answer for him.

As we walk to the office for his appointment, he wants to practise. I see that he is anxious; I don't want nerves to impede the process so I ask simple questions.

"What's your name?"

"Where do you live?"

"What did you do for a living?"

He has no trouble answering and I tell him he'll be fine. I remind him that the notary is a good person who just wants to make sure I don't take off to Mexico with our savings.

"You won't get far on that," he laughs.

The conversation in the office begins well as the notary reviews the purpose of power of attorney agreements, her role, and mine.

"I know I'm having a hard time understanding our money and stuff like that," Lincoln tells her. "I trust Leslie."

I am glad to be sitting to the side and behind him so he cannot see my tears.

She asks the questions we've practised and more. She makes it conversational as they chat about our girls, the weather, and our plans for the winter. He knows what day it is, the season, and the year. He tells her he listens to CBC Radio and watches the news on TV.

"Do you know the name of the prime minister?" she asks.

He hesitates and turns to look at me, a wide-eyed, frightened look. I decide it's okay to give him a clue.

"You don't like him much," I say.

"Stephen Harper!" he says, without missing a beat.

I laugh out loud at the clarity and enthusiasm of his response, and the notary laughs, too. She tells us we can pick up the documents later that week.

I stumble sideways and he catches me in his arms and turns it into a clumsy waltz. I dump my glass of wine and burst into tears. The second glass spills and this time I have to laugh.

If I can't pour it, should I be drinking it?

———————

We go to the annual Christmas party held in the lovingly crafted log home of old friends. Most of our friends live in rural locations, many in houses they built themselves. This one sits high on a hillside, the driveway lit by homemade lanterns—candles glowing inside small paper bags—and the house twinkles with lights. It is movie-set beautiful, right down to the gently falling snow.

Even in small towns, it is possible to go months, even a year or two, without seeing people you know and care about. There will be friends there we haven't seen since our joint diagnoses. Since "before." I know, and Lincoln knows, that everyone there will have heard I have Parkinson's, that he lives with dementia. We are both feeling awkward and self-conscious.

On our arrival, Lincoln is immediately gathered in by a group of men, and I find myself making the rounds, sharing hugs and catching up on everyone's news and plans, just like "before." I remember to sip a cup of wassail slowly. I do the driving now and need to be careful. The road home is long and winding and the snow is still falling.

There are fine musicians among our friends and some beautiful voices to carry the less gifted. We sing carols and the best of our world is manifest in the music and companionship. When I check on Lincoln he is never alone, but taking his place with more ease than I expected, and I am overwhelmed with gratitude for the loving community that is ours.

We stay too long and are both very tired when we arrive back at home. I am chilled and shivering; my whole body is in tremor, out of control. I can't get the key in the lock of the door. Lincoln tries and has no more success than I. Close to tears with weariness and frustration, I look to see if our neighbours' lights are on in case we need to ask for help. I really don't want to have to ask for help. Then I look at him and he grins at me, a goofy, what-the-heck grin . . .

"Shake and Baked!" I say. "That's us, buddy. Shake and Baked."

We are both laughing now. I have no memory of who opens the door, but we don't need to ask for help. We make it inside all by ourselves.

3 Not Lost, Just Going the Wrong Direction

I WANT TO GO HOME. I often think that in the months after my diagnosis with Parkinson's disease. And I think of my dad, and of Lincoln's. Home. Not a physical place but a place of being, a sanctuary of the self, inhabited by confidence and hope, in which the world, or at least one's own small corner of it, makes sense. In my imagined future of walkers and wheelchairs, a frozen gait, a frozen face, and a Swiss cheese brain, I see little hope and I have no confidence. But I am too busy for active despair. The beast is present but I keep it caged. I make rules for my sorrow and for me.

"You can bawl in the shower," I promise myself.

"When Chris takes Lincoln for a walk tomorrow, then you howl. Not before!"

Oh, the beast is present, but I learn to pretend for both Lincoln and myself—for the sake of what must be done—that we have it under control. And this is all happening so quickly. Within a year of our diagnoses, I am relatively unchanged, my symptoms troubling but mild, well managed by the medication I have started to take. My left hand shakes, especially when I am tired or stressed, and my left leg drags when the meds wear off. I don't sleep as well as I used to and the heat bothers me, but my anxiety for myself is largely about the future. Lincoln is changing at nightmare speed. I want to will it all away, to go back to how we were, but no amount of love or effort can hold him in place. Our shared reality is dissolving. He lives more and more in his own confusing world, and the only way to help him is to be with him there. I tell him how much I enjoy the hallucinated "others" in our house, the benign strangers who begin to appear in the daytime, in only his vision.

"They never want a meal or leave the toilet seat up," I tell him. "I like these guys."

He sets extra places at the table and makes them tea. He waits for them to catch up when we hike. You would have to know him to see the humour in that. This is one of the oft-repeated scenes of my life: Lincoln, miles ahead on a cross-country ski or hiking trail, finally thinks that maybe he should stop and wait for me. I puff up to him, exhausted, a little annoyed.

"Great. You're here!" he says as he adjusts his pack and immediately strides off.

Those of us who hike, ski, or bike with him shake our heads at the attentiveness he shows to these new hallucinatory companions. But they become part of our lives; I find myself asking them to watch over him, over us.

We make a new acquaintance, a talented sculptor of wood and stone, a storyteller who wants to leave a written record of his Coast Salish ancestors' origin stories for his children and his children's children. I am honoured to be asked to help him prepare his manuscript for self-publication. We work at our dining room table and Lincoln is often nearby. I have explained to our new friend that Lincoln has dementia, that he sometimes sees people and animals that are not there. Lincoln's hallucinations are nothing out of the ordinary to him. He considers them blessings and tells me that the old ones he sees around my husband enjoy his company very much. That helps me more than I have words to describe.

And just when I think that I am doing well, feeling at home within this new reality, or, rather, this new surreality, Lincoln begins to be confused about who I am.

"Who was that who hopped into my bed last night?"

I want to go home.

I have so much to think about, so much to learn. I become the Queen of Google. I read and read—the websites, the books, the medical articles on both dementia and Parkinson's. I join online Parkinson's support groups and quickly quit most of them. The perky, inspirational voices irritate me and the despairing ones make me sad. I don't want to be a warrior, a hero, or a poster woman. I am not "rocking the disease" or "bravely fighting" it. I am doing the best I can with what I know and I am often terrified.

I watch the videos of the miracle cures and I understand their siren calls, why people spend their money on unproven therapies and supplements, or travel to faraway places for stem cell replacement procedures and electrical stimulation. I learn that, other than the medications with their often horrendous side effects, exercise is the only thing that seems to actually work to mitigate symptoms. I find a personal trainer and begin regular workouts. I buy a treadmill and I use it. Lincoln and I walk and hike and bike. I ask him to dance with me in our living room, and if he doesn't want to, I dance by myself.

And then I meet Jill Carson, a physiotherapist from Sidney, BC. Jill had to give up her practice after her diagnosis with young-onset Parkinson's disease. She and I first connect through an article she posts on the Parkinson's BC Facebook page in the fall of 2012. It is a passionate, frustrated call to action for better treatment and services for those of us living with a neurodegenerative disease for which the gold-standard medication, levodopa, is fifty years old. Jill calls it her "rant" and argues that we need to take a page out of the AIDS activists' playbook, to get organized, to get political, and to get loud—a hard sell to a patient group whose clinical symptoms include fatigue, depression, apathy, and anxiety. It is unlike anything I have read before, and I am energized by her passion and her courage in moving beyond the simplistic "Just stay positive" messages I encounter over and over. I write to Jill and ask how I can help.

"What are you good at?" she asks.

"I like to write," I tell her.

"Those of us with a voice need to use it," she says.

She suggests I think about that, to consider ways my skills might be useful. She shares with me the video she created for the World Parkinson Congress video contest. The congress, the largest international gathering of Parkinson's stakeholders—patients, advocates, caregivers, doctors, support service practitioners, scientists, and pharmaceutical companies—is to be held in Montreal that fall of 2013. Jill, her husband, and one of their daughters are going to Montreal. She invites me to join them. I can't see any way to leave Lincoln, though Jill's enthusiasm inspires me to try to do something. Her challenges seem so much greater than mine, and yet there she is, networking like crazy in order to engage others in the fight for better . . . better understanding, better therapies, better meds, better research, and better communication within the Parkinson's patient community and with the doctors and scientists engaged in our cause. Because of Jill's example, I write a spoken-word piece I call "Parkinshtick" and hire a local high school student to videotape my performance.

I discover, as I write the final few seconds of the piece, that I have reframed, renamed my feelings about living with the disease. Every word is true. It is not great poetry but it is pretty good therapy.

> *You might say, I would agree,*
> *that I've become a trite cliché*
> *of carpe diem glass half-fullness*
> *but this much for sure is true—*
> *it is no virtue but luck or DNA*
> *that holds at bay*

the jackbooted soldiers of depression
when others, wise, kinder, stronger,
must suffer their oppression.
I recognize this gift, this saving grace.
It is the blessing that permits
my determined inner voice.
Embrace this day, she cries.
There is no other choice.

Jill's video makes the top ten list; "Parkinshtick" receives an honourable mention and becomes my Parkinson's party piece. I discover that if I say it really quickly, the whole poem takes only three minutes to recite. People will listen to almost anything for three minutes. I work it first into a short speech I give at a Parkinson Society British Columbia conference and later into another speech, part of the opening celebrations for the Parkinson Wellness Project—Jill's brainchild—a Parkinson's dedicated exercise facility in Victoria.

Jill's rant also inspires a response from Dr. Jon Stamford, a British neuroscientist who is already engaged in Parkinson's research when he develops the disease himself. Jon and I meet online, through Jill. He is producing an e-magazine called *On the Move*, a journal written, edited, and produced entirely by PWPs, or persons with Parkinson's.

The abbreviation PWP, or PwP, depending on who is writing it down, makes me laugh a little when I first encounter it. I keep thinking that it's awfully close to POW, and that is not comforting. I've never gotten used to it and always refer to myself as a "parkie." Some find this term demeaning and I respect that. Jill and Jon both use "parkie," though, and that's confirmation enough for me.

I am impressed by the first issue of *On the Move* that I read, and its theme, romantic love. The stories are well-written first-person narratives, some brutally honest, of relationships strengthened and relationships destroyed when one person in a couple develops the disease.

When Jon invites me to write my stories, I find an outlet for my anxiety. I tell the world, or at least the Parkinson's world, our story, mine and Lincoln's. I receive, in return, empathy and support and I am moved to respond in kind.

In an online patient forum, I read a poignant post written by an American first-grade teacher with thirty-two years' experience: "I tried to qualify for social security disability but have been turned down twice 'because my symptoms don't prevent me from teaching.' I am preparing for my final appeal through a hearing. . . . I loved teaching but getting up at 5:00 AM to have time to get dressed (it is a process since I can't lift my leg up high enough to put on pants). By 9:00 AM it is all I can do to stay alert and not curl up under the reading table and nap. . . . I wish the people that are voting for me to return to the classroom had known me before PD."

I know her. I know her without ever meeting her, without even knowing her name. I know the kind of teacher she is, she was— skilled, kind, dynamic. I am sure of it. On the days Parkinson's kicks me around, I think how hard it would be if I were still teaching. I respond to her with little to offer but sympathy. However, I know where to turn for better and that is to Peggy Willocks, an American educator, a respected Parkinson's advocate, and a member of the editorial board for *On the Move*. Peggy responds immediately to my email and sends me the link to an article she has written on the Social Security disability system. I pass it on via the forum. I don't know how it has gone for this teacher but I do know that her post prompted an outpouring of indignation on her behalf and a number of similar stories, as well as encouragement. And I know Peggy was able to offer proven, practical advice. Others have fought our battles and their successes empower us all.

Jill connects me with Donna, the author of a beautiful collection of meditations on her life with Parkinson's. Because Donna also lives in BC, she, Jill, and I manage to hold several parkie-sisterhood get-togethers. We drink wine, we dance, we laugh, we share our stories. We fill each other up. Reaching out to Jill led me to Jon in England, who led me to Peggy in the American South, and to Dilys—another *On the Move* writer-editor—in New Zealand, whose 1970s backyard wedding pictures remind me very much of my own. Jill, Donna, Jon, Dilys, and I are all in Portland, Oregon, for another World Parkinson Congress in 2016. Jill, Jon, and Dilys are all there in official capacities, as ambassadors from their countries. Donna and I call ourselves "the groupies."

I make new friendships, from all over the world, in a community of brave, inspiring parkies whose honest articulations of their own struggles challenge me to think critically about what it means to be a patient and a caregiver. I am moved to laughter and to tears born of the recognition that something of myself can live in another person's voice and experience.

Once I begin to write, I cannot stop. When *On the Move* folds, I find outlets closer to home, on Facebook, and in in-house magazines for Parkinson's and dementia organizations. I draw strength from the parkie tribe but also from a wider readership of kind hearts who possess a willingness to listen, to try to understand.

Jon Stamford is also invited to speak at the opening of Jill's gym in Victoria. I ask him how he refers to those kind hearts, the ones who don't have Parkinson's.

"Muggles," he says.

I find that hilarious, though I don't know why. Perhaps it is the dark irony or Jon's perfect, deadpan delivery. Or maybe you had to be there.

And maybe, I tell myself, maybe I can write my way home.

When we talk about death, Lincoln always says that he wants to live a good long time but he is not afraid to die.

"I'm curious," he says. "Excited."

"The next great adventure," he calls it.

"Doesn't it bother you not to know?" I ask him. "To not know what's next?"

"No," he says. "That's the whole point of adventures."

We won't be sleeping in the same bed tonight. I will move to the home office, the room right next door, and sleep on the futon. And perhaps we will never ever share a bed again.

I have been away in Vancouver for two nights, attending the Movement Disorders Clinic at the University of British Columbia. Our friend John stayed in our house with Lincoln, who, in my absence, slept well.

"John says you had a good night," I say. "Would you like to sleep alone again tonight?"

"Yes."

Just that, a simple cheerful "yes."

It's just a bed, I tell myself.

Lincoln has always been a night owl, and I, an early-to-bed gal. On the rare nights he found himself in bed before me, he had trouble falling asleep and would wander out to see where I was, to ask me when I was coming to bed. And now he prefers I not join him at all?

Should I be in mourning? I can feel the sorrow, great waves of it, lapping in my inner harbour. After so many years I am not going to be sleeping beside my man, my frustrating, gentle, funny man. To be honest, his restlessness and confusion during the night have been driving me crazy. He hurls himself sideways, ramming his head into my back, tugging sheets, tapping, stealing my pillow.

Sometimes I wake up to find him leaning over me, panicked, trying to puzzle out in the dark just who it is beside him. Should I be in mourning because this is another loss, another heart wound, another reminder that he is slipping away daily, hourly, minute by precious minute? I should be in mourning. And I am. And I am not. I whisper reassurance.

"Hey, buddy. It's me."

He either breathes a sigh of relief and lies back down or sits bolt upright, acutely distressed at finding himself in bed with another woman. I am an awful person for being a tiny bit pleased that he minds so much, the idea of sleeping with someone else. I find it sweet and endearing, but for him it is a nightmare. And as for sex, it fled months and months ago, when the brain cell destruction hit some critical mass, though he was, for a while, obsessed with renewing his Viagra prescription. I tell myself that if I am ever seriously short of cash, I can make a tidy sum of money reselling the packs of little blue pills he has stacked up inside his overnight case.

One night he wakes me up.

"Les. Les . . ."

He stands on my side of the bed looking down at me, grinning broadly, his eyes shining in the dark, a blue pill in one hand and a glass of water in the other.

"For you," he whispers.

"Not happening, buddy."

"Oh. Okay."

Within minutes he is snoring softly beside me while I lie awake for ages and wrestle with amusement and regret.

In the end, it is just a bed. It is a practical solution for a situation that requires a quick resolution. I need to sleep. He needs to sleep. Besides, we are almost always together. I rarely leave him alone, and if I do, it is for the shortest time possible. I am seldom more than a room away from him, twenty-four seven. We touch often. We hold hands when we walk. We always have. I am not over my anger, my fear, my raging against fate, but I am able to pretend to be. That is almost as good. There is no time for self-indulgence and no energy for anything but caring for him and looking after myself. Grief rises. I give it space and time and then try to move it on. I miss him more than I can say.

It's just a bed, I tell myself. *It's just a bed.*

The woman is beautiful. So is the man she is with. I am trying not to stare and I can't tell which one of them has Parkinson's disease. I know one of them does or they wouldn't be here, in the waiting room of the Movement Disorders Clinic at UBC. A name is called and they both stand, or, rather, he stands and helps her to her feet. Now I can tell.

He positions himself in front of her and she grabs on to the back of his belt with two hands as they slowly move out of the waiting room and down the corridor. He walks carefully; she is hesitant and rigid. They are an awkward, two-person conga line, minus the music. It makes me want to cry.

I am not alone—my sister Jane is with me, but Lincoln is not. He is at home, a seven-hour drive away, again in the company of our friend John. Lincoln came with me for my first two visits to the UBC clinic but he is not able to make this trip, or any others. If I cannot be with him, I must arrange for someone else to keep him company, to keep him safe. John is unfazed by the care, willing, and very kind. His sense of humour matches Lincoln's, and this break will be good for both Lincoln and me.

As we wait, I find that I am feeling envious of the beautiful woman, even though she is already struggling in ways I am not, even though I feel ashamed to be reacting this way, even though she must cling to her husband's belt. I assume he is her husband. I am envious because she has a caregiver who loves her—another assumption—because, despite the awkwardness, their moving together has a grace born of practice. And something else. *Tenderness,* I think to myself. *Tender. He tends to her. Tend*erly. When I reach that stage, it won't be my husband with whom I walk; it will be an aluminum walker. That's one hell of a downgrade. *Where is the grace in that? Where is the tenderness?*

I've just completed the depression questionnaire. It's part of the ritual of each visit to the clinic. Parkinson's is a dopamine deficiency disease, and dopamine is the "feel-good" neurotransmitter. Many people with Parkinson's deal with depression, and my neurologist is a caring guy who wants to know if depression is an issue for his patients. Movement disorder is a misnomer. The non-motor symptoms of Parkinson's, the ones that are not obvious, are often more troubling than the tremor, or rigidity, or loss of balance. If you are unaccountably sad or apathetic, or you can't sleep, or you have panic attacks, or all of the above, a tremor or a dragging foot can seem a minor inconvenience. Depression is a big deal but, so far, not my big deal. I hope it stays that way.

An older couple also sits in the waiting room. This time it is obvious who has Parkinson's. Though the disease occurs in men at a slightly higher rate than in women, this is a day for the lady parkies. He holds the clipboard on his lap and quietly reads the depression questions to her. She whispers her answers. I try not to listen. And I envy her, too. Because she has him. Their heads are together, almost touching. He waits for her answers and nods encouragement. He smiles at her even though she cannot smile back. Her face is expressionless, masked by the advanced disease. But, even so, they seem to share the kind of relationship that would normally touch and inspire me, make me feel blessed to have witnessed it. But I don't feel blessed. I am frightened of that place, where she is, where I am probably headed, where my voice will be reduced to a whisper and my smile locked in behind a frozen face. There will be no "he" for me, no gentle, smiling man to read the questionnaire. My world will be very small, perhaps about the size of a room in a long-term care home.

My mother was eighty-four years old when my father died. He was eighty-six. They'd been married for over sixty years. My dad was eighty before Alzheimer's began its cruel erosion of his fine intellect, his memory, and his sense of humour. My mother, a retired nurse, kept him at home and looked after him long past the point where that was reasonable or even safe. It took a bout of pneumonia to put him in the hospital, to take away his ability to walk and, because his doctor would not release him to my exhausted mother, to see him placed in a care facility. When he died, my mother's grief was almost unbearable to witness. Nothing eased her sorrow.

When we visited her as a family, she would look at our girls and say to me, "Oh, how your dad would have loved seeing them." And then she would cry. When I visited alone, her conversation was all about my father, relentlessly about my father. It always left us both in tears. I did not have the heart to say, "No more, Mom. Please, no more."

During one visit I suggested we walk along Dallas Road, a lovely oceanside route right outside the front door of her apartment building.

"Let's walk out along the breakwater," I said. "It's a gorgeous day."

"No," she replied. "I won't do that anymore. There are too many happy couples. I can't bear it."

I was shocked by her answer and by her reason. I didn't understand it then but I do now. Now I know what that kind of grief feels like, now I know how everything can trigger memory, now I know how hard it is not to be consumed by sorrow—or to admit to the possibility of happiness and how disloyal that can feel.

At the time, what I saw as her choice to be unhappy, to stay stuck in her pain, frustrated me. And it was so unlike my mom, a "glass half-full" believer if ever there was one. She had always been the quiet strength in our family, a mother who welcomed her hurting children into her embrace with healing words and infinite patience. She was not perfect but her capacity to love was as close to perfection as any I have ever experienced.

I am not going to do this, I promised myself. I am never going to let my own grief make it impossible for me to be glad that others have joy in their lives, that others might have what I have lost.

Lincoln's illness moves quickly, inhabiting him to the point of childlike dependence within the space of two short years. At the same time, my mother struggles with short-term memory loss, a symptom of her own progressive vascular dementia. At first, I have to tell her over and over that Lincoln is sick, that I have Parkinson's, that's why we aren't visiting as often as we used to.

"Oh, honey," she says each time, "I am so sorry. I should be there with you . . ."

And then she forgets and slips into what I think of as Mom's-missing-Dad-brain-groove. We become what we think, I decide. My mom is wearing pathways in her brain that only lead to sorrow.

Every phone call is the same. Every phone call ends with weeping. I stop saying anything about my Parkinson's. Why put her through that? I mention it only if I am with her and she notices my tremor or my clumsy movement. I can mitigate her distress by minimizing my own, by being cheerful.

"Life is good, Mom," I say. "There are worse things . . ."

I sit in that waiting room with my loving, supportive sister by my side. I spend time with a physiotherapist and then with my neurologist. They both tell me I am doing the right things, that I am doing well. I feel like I did when, as a kid, I got handed a report card full of As. I leave with an adjustment to my medication and some new exercises to challenge my balance and coordination.

When I get home, Lincoln is very happy to see me. He beams and winks when he catches my eye. He follows me from room to room. He pats me, rapid little tap-taps on my head, my shoulders, my knee if we are sitting. He chuckles as he taps. He makes me laugh. He always has. And I love him with a tenderness that astonishes me even as I grieve the loss of all he was.

I think of my mother and the many years when she saw her glass as not only full but overflowing, and this new, sad lesson from the day she would not walk on the breakwater. I find I am grateful for those moments of bitter envy in the waiting room, for what they have revealed to me about myself.

There are worse things than Parkinson's disease. I have only to look around me to see suffering beyond anything I have personally endured. It is not that the hard lives of others disallow my own pain because, by comparison, I have no right to complain. I am okay—not because someone else lives an unhappier life than I do, but because I can choose gratitude. I can choose to be grateful in the same way I choose to love my husband. The way I tender love. Offer. Hold out my hands and say, "Here. This is for you. No matter what comes, this is for you."

And gratitude, the thoughtful counting of blessings, the heart-centred attending to the beauty in the world and the goodness in people—despite all the cliché-ridden coffee cup and wall plaque manifestations of the word—gratitude, this is for me. And this I know. A mind full of gratitude has little room for envy.

Does it sound like I am trying to wear a groove in my own brain? Perhaps I am. And why not? I am my mother's daughter.

He stops suddenly, just as we get to the bottom of the hill. I am relieved to be off the rocky trail. My left foot won't brace like it used to and I slide a lot. We are at a crossing point, just where the descending trail intersects the dirt path that runs along and above the river. I stop, too. The crows in the ponderosas explode into cacophonous flight. I wonder why. Do humans on the move seem more innocent to them than humans at rest? Did our abrupt stopping signal something ominous? I often wonder about crows. They are so cheeky and social. Tough. Confident. Everything I am not these days. I wonder what they know. As suddenly as he stopped, Lincoln starts again. He turns away from me, without a word or a glance, and begins to trot up the path, in the wrong direction. I run to catch up, to get in front of him. A sincere smile is what I need. That and the perfect words.

"Where are you going, honey?" I ask.

"Home," he says and tries to brush past me.

I stand in his way.

"Going the wrong direction," I tell him brightly and then, heartened by the hesitation in his eyes, I carry on.

I know I have to get this right the first time. Perhaps I shouldn't have brought him on such a long walk. I am not used to carrying a cellphone and once again have forgotten it. I don't have a plan for what I will do if he is determined to head upriver. If he decides to go, I will have to go with him. I take silent inventory of the amount of water we have, the snacks, whether or not I packed my meds. I am not used to having to carry them everywhere. I just wanted to take advantage of a beautiful spring morning, to go for a walk. No one knows where we are. I think—I hope—they will look for us here. It's a small town; everyone knows everyone. We often walk this way. Besides, we won't be lost; we will just be going in the wrong direction.

"Look at the river, honey," I say. "See? It's flowing that way. It's going to town. It's going home, like us. See? Remember all those times in the canoe? We put in at Ten Mile and we pulled out at the park. We came this way. The river flows this way. We follow it home. Just like we always have."

I am not used to this. I am not used to living with his rapidly progressing dementia. I am not used to being the one in charge, the boss of both of us. I am not used to living with Parkinson's disease. I am not used to being shaken by tremors and slowed by unresponsive muscles. I am not used to relying on pills. I am not used to his spontaneous episodes of paranoia, his belief that though I look like his wife, I am not she. I am newly a stranger to myself and I hate being a stranger to him. I hate to not be trusted, to not be believed. The irony of it is I do lie to him. I tell him the library is closed sometimes when it isn't, because I don't want him to go alone and he doesn't want me with him. The dementia literature tells me it's okay to do that. It's called "the therapeutic lie." I still feel guilty. I am not used to this.

"Remember that time we hit the rock and I went over the bow? That's just there, honey. Just there. I probably swam right past where we are now. The river would've taken me home if I hadn't been fished out. Let's go home. It's this way. Just like the river."

I see his struggle as I speak. His face flickers with memory and suspicion. Damn. I am losing this one, losing it to derailed synaptic conversations over which neither of us has any control. His face hardens. My panic rises.

Several months earlier my doppelgänger moved into our lives, and out, and in, and out and in, again and again, until just the right dose of the right medication sent her packing—or so I had thought. She introduced herself the first time after a sweet shared nap one dreary winter afternoon.

"Do you have a twin?" Lincoln asked politely.

"Why?"

I chuckled at both the question and the formality in his voice.

"You look just like my wife."

"Oh."

I did not know what to say when he asked why I was crying.

Days later an early morning phone call woke me. It was from Kathy, a close friend. She told me not to worry.

"He's here," she said.

I hadn't even realized he was missing. He had driven our Volkswagen camper eight kilometres up a winding rural highway on summer tires. He hadn't driven in months. I thought I had hidden all the keys.

"He's looking for you. There's a strange woman in your bed. That's what he told us. He's eating a muffin. We'll bring him home."

When he walked in the door, he looked at me with relief.

"There you are!"

He laughed and hugged me. We held on to each other for a long time. I could not help but weep.

"I am just so happy to see you," I told him by way of explanation. "I miss you when you're not here."

"I miss you, too."

That same week, we went to the movies. We had just settled into our seats when Lincoln grabbed his coat and bolted up the aisle. I followed him as soon as I could coax my reluctant left leg into action. He was heading off into the darkness on a bitter cold night, in search of me. Several good friends were just heading into the theatre.

"I need help," I begged. "Stop him."

One friend gently restrained him, held him, spoke calmly. But even so, Lincoln's agitation increased. A 911 call, flashing lights, ambulance attendants, a police car, a tall young cop, and loving faces, bizarrely shining red, then blue, shocked, then sad—and, finally, a curtained room in our small hospital's emergency department. The doctor on call was a gentle man and a familiar face. I stayed out of sight but I listened. I had learned the knack of crying silently.

"You were pretty upset, I understand," the doctor said. "What persuaded you to finally get in the ambulance?"

"Did you see the size of that cop?"

That was what he said.

I learned the knack of laughing silently, too.

And now his stony look of contempt is such an unmistakable signal of where he is at, where we are at, a kilometre and a half from home, alone by the river, with the crows squawking and flapping above our heads. He cannot trust me, but he looks a long time at the river and somehow finds a way to trust it. He turns and heads for home.

"Stay away from me!" he yells.

I jog up ahead and around several bends until I am sure I am well out of his sight. First I check for my Parkinson's pills. There are none. Yes, this really needs to work. I take my sunglasses off and put my hat into my pack. I remove my sweatshirt and tie it around my waist. I make every change to my appearance I can think of. I pace up and down by the side of the trail and wait for him. I take big breaths in and out. The crows are quieter. I guess they do prefer us on the move.

"There you are!" he calls in delight.

"Here I am!"

I walk to meet him. He takes my hand. He complains about the "other one."

"Oh, her," I say. "She's not a problem. She's just not reliable."

"Not like you," he teases.

"Not like me."

4 More Than I Ever Wanted to Know

LINCOLN, OUR FRIEND LEORA, AND I have been hiking together for a while, a habit that began in the early days of his illness. I am reassured to have someone else along, someone who loves us and is easy and relaxed with his hallucinations. Sometimes Leora and I chat as we walk, and Lincoln seems to enjoy listening to our conversation. Other times our talking seems to stress him, especially during the difficult months of the "other Leslie." I never have to apologize or explain to Leora why we need to walk in silence, and she is almost as quick as I am in picking up his cues. She is good company for both of us. A widow of many years, raising her daughter on her own, she understands my grief.

One of our favourite routes takes us into the hills above a subdivision just to the east of town. The shortest way to access the trail is through the strands of a barbed wire fence, at the point where they are attached to a sturdy post, an easy enough climb, even for me. We aren't trespassing, just saving some time and steps, as there is a gate farther along the fenceline.

This afternoon, after a long, pleasurable hike, we arrive back at the fence. I am on one side, Leora on the other, and Lincoln is stuck between, straddling the bottom wire, while one of us or maybe both spread the wires to give him as much space as possible.

He is bent at the waist, one hand on the post, a leg on either side of the fence, and he doesn't move. He stares at the ground, unconcerned and unresponsive, frozen, as if he had been captured in a photograph. In actual time it may be seconds or maybe it is longer. It feels like forever. We are unable to help him physically, as he is stiff and rigid, or guide him with our words—he doesn't seem to hear us—though we try.

It is a bizarre occurrence, this physical freezing and mental disappearing act, but it turns out to be the first of many such occurrences. Cognitive fluctuations that can also affect motor function are characteristic of Lewy body dementia. As Lincoln hangs on the fence, I know nothing about Lewy body dementia, but soon I will learn a great deal. Parkinson's disease, I am to discover, has a lot in common with Lewy body dementia.

In the early 1900s, a German neurologist, Friedrich H. Lewy, was doing research on the brains of deceased Parkinson's patients. He discovered abnormal aggregations or clumping of a protein called alpha-synuclein, later named Lewy bodies. Lewy bodies in the brain stem disrupt the production of dopamine. Both Parkinson's disease and Lewy body dementia are dopamine deficiency diseases. About fifty percent of Parkinson's patients will go on to develop Parkinson's-related dementia, also known as dementia with Lewy bodies, usually ten to twenty years after diagnosis with Parkinson's. As their disease progresses, people with Lewy body dementia often develop physical parkinsonisms, including tremor, slowness of movement, balance impairment, and rigidity.[1]

The Coles Notes version might go something like this:

It's all about the timing.

Physical symptoms first, that's Parkinson's.

Dementia symptoms first, that's Lewy body dementia.

Hallucinations and experiencing a loved one as an imposter typically occur early in the progression of Lewy body dementia and later in other dementias. This "gone-away" state, however, this transient loss of consciousness, is specific to Lewy body dementia. Those night terrors Lincoln has been experiencing for several years now, they have a name: REM sleep behaviour disorder. RSBD for short—another acronym to add to the growing list. RSBD is often a predictor that Lewy body dementia lurks somewhere in a patient's future.

When he returns to himself, and to us, he squeezes though the fence and straightens up. He calmly takes the lead as if nothing has happened. I think, for him, nothing has.

"What was that all about?" Leora whispers.

"I don't know," I say. "I am so glad I wasn't alone."

Then we follow him down the hill and back to town.

It is hard to get truly lost in and around Grand Forks. Climb high enough and you can always find the rivers. However, there are better or safer routes to follow, and Lincoln's once excellent sense of direction becomes increasingly confounded as his dementia progresses. He is used to being the wayfinder on our wanderings, and I have always been content to follow. In the past he sometimes encouraged me to take the lead, more for the entertainment provided by my confusion than from any desire to share his role as head guide.

"What would you do if you were here by yourself?" he would laugh when I stopped to puzzle out where to go next.

"I wouldn't be here by myself!" I always answered.

But now, though he is accurate in his sense of the general direction, the routes he picks are not always practical, not always safe. He seems more and more to be guided by what he can see in the distance, the river below or a hilltop above, and his inclination is to follow a direct route down to the valley bottom or up to a crest, regardless of the obstacles in the way. He wants to go as the crow flies—though cliffs and rocky outcroppings, barbed wire fences, tangles of bushes, or clumps of trees, ponds, and creeks may stand in the way.

When Leora and I suggest alternate routes, he is annoyed, sometimes telling us to choose our own path and let him choose his. If I have to, I plead Parkinson's, and he is too kind to persist, grudgingly accepting that we might have to retrace our steps or follow a longer route to our destination. He is also plagued by the hallucinations that grow less benign as his frustration increases.

"These darn kids!" he complains.

"What are they doing, honey?"

"Pesking . . . pesketing . . ."

"Pestering you?"

"Yes!"

"Shall I use my teacher voice and send them on their way?"

"Yes!"

"Enough of this, you guys!" I shout. "I mean it."

I issue commands in a tone I hardly ever used in the classroom. The irony of it is that Lincoln hated my teacher voice and always objected when I used it on our girls.

"Leave us alone!" I tell these figments of his poor, disordered brain. "Go home NOW!"

"You know," I tell him, as he checks over his shoulder to make sure they are not still following, "they just want to be where you are. You're everyone's favourite librarian."

And he is.

A nursery monitor sits on the bedside table, right next to my pillow. I sleep lightly, new-mother sleep, every sense tuned to changes in his breathing, the rustling of bedclothes, and especially the sound of his feet hitting the floor. I can go from sleep to running in a single second and my nights are peppered with hits of adrenalin.

He can't find his way to the bathroom so I light the route with night lights, one in the bedroom near the door, one in the hallway above the baseboard, and another in the bathroom, which is just steps away at the end of the hallway. I am pleased with the arrangement when I first set it up.

"Look, honey," I tell him. "I've made you a runway. You'll be able to find the bathroom now."

When sounds from the monitor pull me from a rare deep sleep, I fly into the bedroom to find him naked, crouched in the middle of the bed, wide-eyed and panicked.

"Oh, buddy," I say. "What's going on?"

He is unable to answer but stares at the wide rectangular mirror that hangs over our dresser. The lights from my cleverly designed "runway" reflect the room and his body shape. To my eyes, it looks weird, nightmarish, like a threatening, hulking ghoul is in the room. I can only imagine how it must look to him. As I reach for him on the bed, my feet splash through a puddle on the floor. Pee. Pee everywhere. Pee soaking the top sheet lying half off the bed and his pyjama bottoms on the floor. Pee running under the bed. And now the tears come—and all the anger born of unrelenting exhaustion and sorrow.

"There's pee everywhere!" I holler. "Everywhere! You have to call me, Lincoln! I'll always come! You have to call me! Why won't you call me?"

I rage and sob as I bundle up the wet sheet and pyjamas and dump them in the washing machine, as I fill a bucket with water, as I wipe up the pee on my hands and knees, still in the bizarre half-light of the night lights. I stand up too quickly and my head swims. I sit on the edge of the bed with my head between my knees while the dizziness passes, then storm out of the room to the linen closet to get a clean sheet. I fling it on the bed. I yank open a drawer and grab a pair of pyjama bottoms and fling those on the bed, too. I am quiet now but still seething as I help him into his pyjama bottoms, as I remake the bed.

"Where's your T-shirt?" I ask.

He cannot answer.

"Never mind," I mutter.

I get a clean T-shirt and slip it over his head. He is at least able to find the armholes and finish dressing himself.

"Lie down," I order and cover him with the sheet.

"I can't do this," I tell him.

I am drowning in self-pity. I could school Saint Stephen himself in martyrdom.

"You have to call me!"

"You have no idea," he whispers after a moment, his words so soft I can barely hear them.

I have no idea. I have no idea. Now I am drowning in remorse and sobbing.

"I'm sorry. I'm so sorry. Oh, honey, I'm so sorry."

"It's hard for you, too," he says, and he opens the sheet, inviting me in.

I crawl in beside him, curve around him, find the familiar, sweet melding of my body to his. He is asleep in seconds but I lie awake for a long time. In the morning, I hang a tablecloth over the mirror. The obvious symbolism does not escape me as I disappear from my own view.

Good, I think. *Enough with looking at yourself.*

I do what I can to try to make life easier for him and to keep him safe, spending hours on the computer researching dementia and strategies for caregivers. I consider shoes with GPS systems and put alarms on our front and back doors. I learn that the changes in vision that occur with dementia can make it hard for some patients to see white. Staff in care facilities discovered this—their male residents were peeing in the garbage can, even when it was right beside the toilet—so some bright soul wondered if a black toilet seat might help, and it did, for some. Though he isn't peeing in the garbage can, not yet, I am attempting to be proactive, to stay one step ahead of the changes.

It's worth a try, I think, and I begin sourcing black toilet seats. It takes a couple of weeks for our local hardware store to find one and order it in. They're not a popular item. That's no surprise.

By the time it arrives and our friend Chris has installed it for us, another problem arises. Lincoln is now frightened by the transition bar that covers the join where the wooden floor of the hallway meets the tiles on the bathroom floor. He is not able to tell me what he sees but the literature is full of examples. The theory is that dementia sufferers perceive these disruptions in floor patterns as gaps or crevices. Chris finds a replacement that more closely matches the colour of the wooden floor and Lincoln stops hesitating at the bathroom door. A small victory but one that is hard to celebrate. His nighttime incontinence has now reached the point where the only solution is the indignity of adult diapers.

I try to tell myself that dignity, or the lack thereof, is a matter of perception, that I can change how he . . . how I . . . feel about this by changing my thinking. Does it matter where he pees so long as it's contained? Pee is just pee. We all pee. Why does wearing a diaper feel so degrading when perching on a toilet seat does not? Is it because babies wear diapers? Everyone loves babies. Do we stop loving each other, caring for each other, because we age out of cuteness? He needs the diapers. Through no fault or choice of his own, he needs them. Big deal.

I cannot talk myself into a gracious acceptance of the diapers. I try. I want to. I just cannot get there.

"You can relax at night," I tell him. "You won't have to worry about making it to the bathroom. That's a good thing, right?"

Lincoln accepts the diapers with sorrow—and with grace. And once again, because he can, I must. Sometimes I wonder who is caring for whom.

One day, in the liquor store, I find myself juggling more bottles of wine than I can manage.

"Oh, oh," I say aloud.

A nice, youngish man comes to my rescue. He swoops in and tries to grab the bottle threatening to wobble its way out of my left hand. Instead of letting go of the bottle, I clutch it tightly and dramatically to my chest. The Parkinson's brain is a funny thing and often there is a disconnect between the intention and the message that miscreant neurons send to the rest of the body. It's called dystonia and it is not cool. Nice Man, dear heart that he must be, looks a little perplexed but hangs on, still determined to save both me and my wine, despite the fact that his hand, my hand, and the Ehrenfelser are slammed close to my left boob.

"I have a thing," I stammer. "Just give me a moment."

And he does.

I try to speak politely to people, even when I am upset, and my wayward body parts deserve the same courtesy. After all, they really aren't in control. Nothing is in control. That's the nature of the beast.

Hand, I silently plead. Big breath and then another. *Hand, you can let go now.*

My hand relaxes. Nice Man saves the wine and we walk side by side to the till.

"Thank you," I say. "I have Parkinson's disease. It can be weird."

He smiles and returns to complete his shopping. I walk home, just a few short blocks, but long enough to give me time, time to decide to laugh or cry. It makes a much better story for Lincoln if I laugh.

He sits in his chair in the dining room of our Grand Forks house. It is a room full of light, much more a gathering place than the gloomy living room across the hall. Before he got sick, he rarely sat down in the daytime, but now he sits often, drifting into sleep or just staring out the windows. I am busy around him, always conscious of my bustling and wondering if it bothers him.

I am busier than before, not only because of the care he requires but because he used to do so much. Ours was a division of labour worked out without discussion or negotiation; it simply evolved. I cooked, he washed dishes; I scrubbed bathrooms, he vacuumed. He did the laundry and I sorted and folded and put it away. I hated grocery shopping but he read flyers and made lists and paid attention to whether or not we were running low on laundry soap or toilet paper. He chose fruits and vegetables carefully and checked till receipts for errors. And he found them. Not once have I ever bothered to check a till receipt. And I am embarrassed to confess to how much bitter celery and how many mouldy oranges I have packed home and thrown out in the days of his illness and after.

But now he sits in the chair and I hardly ever leave him alone. He and I go grocery shopping together and he pushes the cart and waits quietly while I choose what to put in it.

"Is this a good one?" I ask and pass him a grapefruit.

He takes it in his hands and his face shows his bewilderment. I take it from him and put it in the cart.

"Thanks, honey," I say. "I am sure it's a good one."

And so it goes. Every day a hundred small confusions and every day they change. A week ago, or even yesterday, he might have tested the weight of the grapefruit in one hand and checked the texture of the skin. He might have sniffed it, and if I had chosen it, he would have returned it to the pile and picked another, just to bug me. I can't keep up and I cannot bear to think how quickly I am losing him. I cannot bear to think how it must be for him.

He sits in his chair and looks defeated. I see in his eyes such desolation.

"You look sad," I say. "Are you sad?"

"I am," he answers. "But I am fighting it."

The phone call comes in the spring of 2013. It is from an editor at Orca Book Publishers, a well-respected, BC-based publisher of children's books. They have accepted a manuscript of mine for publication, a picture book entitled *In the Red Canoe*. Lincoln is nearby as I gush my excitement and gratitude. I hang up the phone and, true to form, dissolve in a mess of tears. There is more to it, though, than finally, after rejection upon rejection, being able to say "my book."

I wrote the first draft several years earlier, at a time when I was starting to long for grandkids and had no idea if, or when, they might be part of our lives. Dementia and Parkinson's were not even remotely imagined possibilities. I daydreamed scenarios in which Lincoln and I share our old red canoe with our children's children, showing them all the extraordinary natural wonders best experienced by quiet paddle strokes and slow drift, the magical things that had been part of their mothers' young lives—a dragonfly's iridescent wings, that moment of breathless suspense before an osprey plunges to the water, frogs, ducklings, minnow schools, and the swallows' sundown dancing.

And so I wrote a poem, in which each verse, or pair of verses, held an image of its own, and a memory. I tweaked and added and changed things, and when an editor at Orca expressed conditional interest based on a rewrite, I tweaked and added and changed some more.

When I first met Lincoln he was driving an orange Volkswagen camper with a red canoe on top, a canoe he'd made himself. I used to tell him I fell in love with the van and the canoe, that he was the bonus. The summer of 1976, our first summer together, we canoed the Bowron Lakes circuit. This extraordinary loop of five connected lakes in the Cariboo Chilcotin region of British Columbia is a canoeist's dream. However, our new relationship barely survived the first two days of long, muddy, hot, mosquito-infested portages, each of which we hiked three times, totalling over twenty kilometres. First we carried in our gear—packs loaded with our tent, sleeping bags, food, clothing, tools, stove, axe, cooking pots, and dishes, before caching it all high in bear-proofed trees. Then we slogged back to the trailhead to pick up the canoe and carry it in.

Bug-bitten, itchy, grumpy, sore, and exhausted by the time we made camp, I took it out on Lincoln. He grumped back, and if turning around had meant anything other than redoing all those hideous portages, I suspect both our trip and our relationship could have ended then and there. On the third day, we mercifully settled into what became two weeks of tranquil paddling, punctuated by one white-knuckled whitewater run we executed beautifully.

It seems like there might be a metaphor for our relationship in there somewhere. It is definitely a pattern—we hit a rough patch and treat each other badly but carry on because we have so much work invested in staying together. And we love each other. After a few rough days, we apologize and return to a place of calm waters and easy paddling, with just enough excitement to keep things interesting. I love metaphors and am good at stretching them. I think this one works for us.

One morning, we paddled round a bend and came face to knees with a huge cow moose. From my seat in the bow I looked straight up at her as she bobbed her massive head up and down. I had a few brief seconds in which to think about how funny she looked, as if she were checking us out through bifocal lenses and having trouble finding the focus point. But moose have long legs and sharp hooves, and my next thoughts were about how quickly she could be on top of us, should she so choose. I began a fear-fuelled back-paddle while Lincoln, juggling his camera and paddle, protested.

"No! No! I want to get a picture of her."

Ah, the story of our lives—Lincoln boldly urging me on while I, imagining worst-case scenarios, back up. I call it being sensible. He calls it no fun.

He paddled to and I paddled fro while the moose bobbed and huffed indignant breaths in our direction. I don't remember exactly how it all ended; it was that long ago. I know there is a picture of her, not a very good one, by Lincoln's fine photographic standards. It's hard to get a good shot from a moving canoe.

I often think of that moose moment and know for sure there is a metaphor in there. We did not always paddle in the same direction. We often worked at cross-purposes but we always managed to stay in the canoe. The memory, like the photograph, might be fuzzy and a little out of focus but I treasure it. It makes me laugh. And then it makes me cry.

Laura Bifano, the talented artist who illustrated *In the Red Canoe*, has never met Lincoln or me, but her beautiful pictures touch my heart every time I look at them. Laura's grandpa looks much like Lincoln, and the child in the canoe could easily be our daughter Sarah as a little girl.

That old canoe is now brittle and faded. At this very moment it rests on a pair of sawhorses in Naomi's backyard, awaiting a fresh coat of red paint. Its whitewater days are over but it is still waterworthy enough for a calm lake on a summer day. Lincoln and I won't be in it but our girls will be, and those grandchildren I once wished for, they will be, too. The canoe will once again carry those I love into quiet and beautiful places. Of all the submissions that I have ever sent to publishers of children's books, and there have been many, *In the Red Canoe* would be the one I would most hope to find acceptance.

In December 2013 Lincoln and I "camp" in our sparsely furnished new condo in Revelstoke for our first long visit. We purchased the condo in September at the urging of our daughters; it is conveniently located just steps away from each of their houses. Our girls have been driving winding roads and mountain passes to visit us. Both travel with babies, our grandsons, and I am sick with worry each time they are on the road. Having the condo means an eventual end to all that travel for them and answers the question of where we will live as our illnesses progress.

There is a lot of snow in the valley, and not much sun, but Revelstoke is a beautiful little town and our new neighbours are kind and welcoming. We go easily between the girls' houses and our new home. I know that a permanent move here makes sense for so many reasons, the biggest of which is to be part of our grandchildren's lives, but I cannot call this home. Not yet.

I wake to a morning that promises the first bright sun in weeks. Golden light spills slowly over mountaintops, first gilding Mount

Begbie's glaciers and then Macpherson's snow-crusted dome and the giant handprint on its flank the locals call the Fingers. As the sun rises, snow dazzles from jagged peaks that pierce a sky so clean and crisp and blue it seems polished. I fill the little camera I purchased with Air Miles points with picture after picture. Then I stand, coffee mug in hand, shivering on a balcony that gives view to all this glory. Lincoln joins me.

"I need a better camera," I say.

"Why?" he asks. "It's all right here in front of you."

After spending a month over Christmas in the Revelstoke condo, we return home to Grand Forks in mid-January. One evening, I leave half my dinner on the plate and tell Lincoln I am full. He points to the empty chair beside him.

"Maybe she would like it," he says.

When I start in with my usual, "I think that's a brain trick; there's no one . . ." he laughs.

"Just kidding!" he says, cracking himself up, and me, too.

The next day we drive to Castlegar to deal with a minor recall issue for our vehicle. While we wait for the car to be serviced, he tells me that we were at Nancy Greene Lake before he figured out it was me driving. The Nancy Greene turnoff is sixty-eight kilometres from home.

"Who did you think it was?" I ask him.

He shrugs and smiles. Then he tells me he wants to videotape the people he can see that no one else can. He is so calm when he says these things, and saying anything is becoming harder for him. He is showing symptoms of aphasia now, the progressive loss of speech, and another marker of dementia, though, as with his freezing at the fence, I don't understand at the time what is going on. All I know is that the changes are happening quickly and I am scrambling frantically to keep up.

That same week I leave him alone for a short time while I run errands. When I return home he accuses me of being an imposter.

"Where is she?" he demands.

I suggest he call our close friends Kathy and Chris for reassurance that I am the real Leslie. Their conversation helps, as does a long, long hug.

"See," I say. "This good feeling . . . that's because it's me."

We talk more about "brain tricks" and he tells me he is seeing things, "fluffs," he calls them, drifting in and out of his vision. Dr. Google explains these are probably floaters but could be indicators of small rips in the back of his eye. I make an appointment with our optometrist to have them checked out. The "fluffs" are indeed floaters, and I hope they become less bothersome now that he knows they are not harmful, if only he can remember that.

The very next day he makes that early morning drive in the Volkswagen Westfalia to Kathy and Chris's house, the trip he took to search for me because the "other Leslie," the wrong one, was asleep in our bed. She is becoming a real pain in the ass! After Kathy and Chris bring Lincoln home, he lets me take him to the hospital where our family doctor is on call. He does a thorough neurological examination and orders blood work to rule out infection. He repeats what I have been saying about absolutely no driving, and Lincoln nods his agreement. I know he has no choice but his graciousness with all this out-of-control change is remarkable. It is his example that holds me together.

Our doctor agrees that the move to Revelstoke is a good idea, since there must be a move, no matter what. Our lovely old house and big lot are high maintenance. So am I. So is Lincoln. The doctor suggests back-and-forth travel is confusing for him and that the next trip to Revelstoke should be a permanent move.

Okay, I think. *I can do this. After all, we already have a place to live there.*

The big sorrow, at the time, is abandoning plans to visit my mom in Victoria. I tell myself that I will get us settled in Revelstoke as soon as possible, that I will get respite care sorted out for Lincoln, and then I will visit my mother. A few months, I think, not the fifteen it will actually take. Sometimes it is a blessing not knowing what the future holds.

———————

My plan to move to Revelstoke in the spring of 2014 crumbles as the winter unfolds in a nightmare of confusion and paranoia for Lincoln. I cannot imagine putting him through the turmoil of packing and moving, so I make the decision to remain in the Grand Forks house. I don't know how, or when, we will move. I know I am losing him far more quickly than anyone predicted. Throughout that winter and into the spring, I struggle with managing his paranoia, his confusion around the "real Leslie" and the imposter. It takes time to figure out that a tiny amount of an antipsychotic medication eases the paranoia. Getting him to take it is difficult. How can he be expected to accept pills from a woman he does not trust and sometimes fears? He refuses the pills, so I crush them in the bathroom and secrete them in my left hand—which is pretty curved in all the time now anyway, like a claw—and then hide them in his food.

When we finally settle on a liquid form that I can slip into his juice, I feel like Lucrezia Borgia and am terrified he will catch me in the act of doctoring his beverages. I know the drug can cause complications for someone with dementia and try to use the smallest amount possible. Dementia patients are particularly vulnerable to nasty side effects from mood-altering drugs, and I am careful with my dosages. Maybe too careful? Maybe not careful enough?

We have good health-care professionals helping us, but no one is a specialist in dementia disorders and all have huge caseloads. I write to a number of neurologists who treat dementias but all have long waiting lists. We are talking years, not weeks or months. Even if I could find a specialist and make an appointment, travel with Lincoln is problematic, and he tells me, "No more doctors." How am I to manage his care while respecting his wishes and granting him as much autonomy as possible? What are the best decisions for him? For me? It is a big bus I am driving. Sometimes I manage to keep the bus on the road and sometimes we blow a tire or hit the ditch.

My friends Kathy and Tracey are with me one evening soon after the awful night at the movie theatre. Lincoln's mistrust spreads from me to them. He wants to go for a walk, alone, late at night, and we lock the doors and hide the keys.

"Get out of here!" he orders. "And take your goons with you!"

Goons! I don't know whether to laugh or cry. I may do both. Days later he challenges me again.

"You're up to something," he says. "Where is she?"

I suggest we look at photo albums.

"Ask me anything about any place or any person," I say. "Ask me things only the real Leslie would know."

And so he pulls album after album off the shelf and I point and explain and answer every question he asks. When I can't be stumped, he slams the last album shut and looks me in the eye, a long, hard look.

"Oh, you're good," he says. "You're really good."

5 *More Than I Ever Wanted to Feel*

LINCOLN IS ON THE PHONE to Chris, complaining about the other Leslie and her continued presence in our house. Kathy emails me to let me know she will stay home in case I need her. When this confusion takes hold, speaking to one of our trusted friends can sometimes reset Lincoln's perception of reality. However, the opposite also occurs and the web of mistrust widens to include our friends, as well. This time I am lucky and able to get through to him, once again, with a good, long hug.

"Your brain plays this trick on you and mine makes me shake and stumble. What a pair we are!" I tell him. "Wouldn't the world be horrified if there really were two Leslies?"

He laughs at that.

I don't know what the trigger was but I was out of the house for less than half an hour. Maybe that, or not enough exercise, or just a neuron—or ten—misfiring. Never a straight pitch. Always a curveball.

———

I write to my brother and sisters. I have told them about the incident at the movie theatre and I know they are worrying about us. It has become almost impossible to talk on the phone, and I understand why it upsets Lincoln. Overhearing himself discussed must feel awful. Email has become my primary method of communication.

Dear Sibs,

Try not to worry about us. It gets easier. It gets easier. New realities. I just didn't see this coming. Though I guess, with all the "others" in the house these past months, I might have anticipated it.

It's a symptom, in the dementia literature, thinking the spouse is an imposter.

Yesterday at the dentist he was very concerned that I was paying the bill with Visa as "Leslie likes to collect the points."

It took a while to figure out, since I was paying with Visa, but then, of course, he didn't think I was Leslie, the real Leslie.

"It's okay," I said. "These will automatically go on her account."

Problem solved.

The rest of the day I got to be me, "good" Leslie. I am seeing a definite pattern with even the most benign change or stress triggering confusion. He was ready for the dentist twenty minutes early and all set to walk downtown himself. Later, he called me "my friend." Beats "imposter" by a whole lot!

Love you so much,

L

Hi Kath,

We are going to pass on your birthday party. I know you understand. I am most worried about his violent hiccups. They happen almost every night now and the conversation will be too much for him. We will do something lovely for you, just the four of us, when we can.

Please ask Chris not to bring it up with Lincoln when they go for their walk today. He initially said he wanted to go to your party "because he should" but it's not a good idea for anyone, not just Lincoln. I want you to enjoy your dinner and not be worried about us. I would be a bit of a stress case, even if I could pull out my best acting chops.

Love,

L

Lincoln wakes early one morning, at six o'clock. He usually sleeps until about eight, and I enjoy my quiet, solitary starts to the day. Early rising usually forebodes some troubled times, so I am vigilant and anxious. He tells me that when he went to bed, "everything was backwards."

"Backwards at bedtime?" I ask him.

"Yes."

"Is it backwards now?"

"Well . . . no, but some are."

"So I guess it's a good thing you're an old hippie and can handle things like that."

"Yes," he chuckles.

"Imagine if you were a square peg in a square hole all your life—think how upsetting this backwards stuff would be."

That makes him laugh. "It's sort of like a . . ." He searches for words. "A such in such in such in such."

I cannot help but laugh. And he laughs as well, all the while scolding me for laughing.

Later, we FaceTime with our daughter Sarah and our grandson Arlo, who is almost two. This is part of most mornings and a lovely piece of our day, as is our time with Naomi and our other grandson, Theron, later in the afternoon.

Lincoln is intrigued by what he can see of Sarah's home on the computer screen. "She has a nice place," he says. "I've never seen it before."

It's raining and our house is gloomy, and I think perhaps his weariness from getting up so early and not being able to walk because of the rain are taking their toll on his mood. He begins to pace and ask about the "old worries"—the other Leslie, how the bills get paid, his car keys, where his parents are.

"I'm worried about my sister," he tells me.

I say what I always say when he talks about Christine. "She's with your Mom and Dad, honey. They'll look after her. She doesn't hurt anymore."

And I am learning. I am learning. I am learning a lot of distraction strategies to help us through these moments. We need to go for groceries and he is insistent we go *now*. When we get to the car, I suggest a drive to give the engine "a bit of a workout." The truth is that I need some time to assess things—can we go for groceries or do I need to call on friends for help in calming him down?

We drive the North Fork loop, a winding two-lane highway that follows the Granby River, sixteen kilometres up one side and sixteen down the other, crossing at a single-lane bridge. It's a beautiful route and one he has driven, biked, and rollerbladed many times, probably hundreds of times. I comment on the new green on the willows.

"Nature's first green is gold," I say, and then I recite the whole poem, Robert Frost's "Nothing Gold Can Stay."

> Nature's first green is gold,
> Her hardest hue to hold.
> Her early leaf's a flower;
> But only so an hour.
> Then leaf subsides to leaf.
> So Eden sank to grief,
> So dawn goes down to day.
> Nothing gold can stay.

"That's nice," he says. "Did you just make that up?"

There are newborn calves in the fields and Lincoln is calm and smiling. I can relax. We are going to be all right, for a little while, anyway. He is enjoying the drive and so am I, despite the persistent drizzle. Highland cattle are loose by Hummingbird Bridge—gorgeous shaggy beasties with spectacular horns. There is no other traffic so we can dawdle. We roll down our windows to get a closer look, and they come near enough to touch. It makes him nervous, and that makes me sad. In times past, he would have had his camera out and gotten right into those furry faces, clicking away. As we pass the Snake Hole turnoff, a dirt road that leads to a favourite beach near town, I say, "That was nice. It's been a while."

"I've never seen some of that country before," he tells me.

Lincoln and I are watching *Frozen* on TV. At least I am. Lincoln is dozing. He wakes up and looks around.

"What's up, honey?" I ask.

"I need the bathroom."

"Okay."

He chuckles. Sits there.

"Aren't you going to go now?"

"That's just it."

"What is?"

"I don't . . . don't . . ."

"You don't know where it is?"

"That's it."

I walk him to the bathroom. He looks at it with surprise.

"It's exactly the same," he says.

"What do you know," I say.

Dear Kath,

This was our afternoon . . . lunch, nap, get ready to walk. On our way out the door Lincoln says "See you later" to the invisible whomever in our dining room. It is pouring rain so we come in and decide to watch a movie. 12 Years a Slave *and* Nebraska *are both on Shaw On Demand but Lincoln says, "Leslie would like to see those," and we can't watch them without her. So we watch* All Is Lost.

Enough said.

L

———————

Lincoln asks me about the car keys.

"I have them, honey," I say.

I explain again, as kindly as I can, that the doctor thinks it's a good idea if I do all the driving. He nods. Later he brings me the basket in which he used to keep his keys, and I explain again about him not driving. This time his eyes fill up with tears.

I do manage to say, "I know this is so hard," and he lets me hug him. Between us, we find a way back to being okay. What will I do if we can't find our way back? What will I do?

He falls asleep in his chair, startles awake, and goes down to the basement, returning with an empty ice cream pail.

"What is that for?" I ask him.

"For Sarah," he says. "She's sick."

He has remembered that our daughter Sarah is having an uncomfortable pregnancy with lots of vomiting. I explain that she is visiting in Victoria, and he kind of laughs at himself but he heads to the basement three more times—once to return the bucket, once to go and get another, and once to return it again—before the feeling that she needs the bucket goes away.

Something I once read, and have never been able to find again, mentions the "angel self" that is sometimes revealed through the dementia process. I can't put words to what the writer meant but it lives in my heart, that phrase. There is an honesty in his reactions, as if he has lost all ability to dissemble or to conceal his feelings. He is transparent in his affections. I am not the only one to be brought to tears by the sweetness of his smile. For all that he has lost, for all the frustration he must endure, he ought to be raging but he is not. He is open, and gentle, and kind. I think he has a pretty large "angel self." Lucky me.

I am preparing for a trip to Vancouver, for an appointment at the UBC Movement Disorders Clinic. John is once again going to stay with Lincoln.

"Tell me again," Lincoln says.

"The plan for this week?"

"Yes."

"Well, today John and Mary Ann are coming for dinner," I explain. "Then John is going to spend the night."

"Right."

"Right. It's a practice run so we know everything will be okay when I go to Vancouver on Wednesday."

"You're coming back?" he asks.

"Yes, of course, on Friday. It's all on the paper."

"Right. You're coming back."

"Of course. You're my guy!"

I pause before continuing.

"That is the answer you want to hear, isn't it? That I am coming back?"

I am laughing now. I don't know if he joins me simply because my laughter is contagious or he gets the joke. It doesn't matter.

"'Cause you're stuck with me, pal. But while I'm in Vancouver seeing my Parkinson's doctor, John will be here with you."

"I won't be alone?"

"No, honey, never alone."

"Good!" he sighs. "Because someone needs to know how to run that darn TV."

Once upon a time, not so very long ago, my husband was a strong swimmer, tackling whitewater runs in the canoe and kayak without fear. I sat on river beaches, my heart in my mouth, and watched him as he practised rolling and righting his kayak. With a flick of his hips he could tip himself upside down into the water, the kayak's gleaming bottom all I could see for what seemed a long time, too long. Then, just as I was about to leap to my feet and run to the water to effect a rescue I had no idea how to accomplish, he would bob upright, dripping and grinning, and raise his paddle to me in salute.

But now he has forgotten how to swim and clings to the dock in panic. John coaxes him to move hand over hand to the ladder and up the rungs to safety. Why did I assume he could still swim when so much else has been taken from him?

I have rented Mary Ann's family cabin on Christina Lake for a week, and the girls and their families travel from Revelstoke to join us. I think this is likely to be our last holiday all together, and I long for something memorable to stand against the erosion of family and the breaking of our hearts. The plan is that Lincoln and I will stay at home and commute to the cabin each day. Nighttimes are tricky enough without a change in environment to add to his confusion.

Sometime later, Naomi contacts many of his friends and asks them to write a story or two about their experiences with her dad. She compiles them all, adds photographs, and binds them into a book of memories that we can read to him. In a piece called "Lincoln the Lifesaver" our friend Martin writes:

Not too many people know of Lincoln's heroics on the Granby River. We were a ragtag group of kayakers who loved to head up the Granby in the spring and paddle a section about fifty-two kilometres from Grand Forks. The canyon run was about ten kilometres long and full of surf waves, raging rapids, and nasty keeper holes. We tempted fate every time we ventured out on that whitewater. Lincoln survived some long, cold swims through menacing rapids and dangerous boulder fields. None of us had rock solid rolls so everyone swam on a regular basis.

We became fairly proficient at rescues.

One particular paddle we started a few kilometres above the canyon to warm up. The sun was out and the water was fast and brown with runoff. Rounding a bend in the river, a large logjam came into view just as Rob took the lead. He was on it quickly and in a very dangerous situation, with no way to go without the risk of being swept under. Lincoln and I decided to beach our boats and swim across to the jam to try and extricate Rob. Being on a logjam in high water is not a wise move but the only way to get to Rob was to dance across it to where he sat in his boat and lift him, boat and all, out of the water and onto the jam. Without Lincoln's help and disregard for his own safety, Rob would have been left in a very precarious position.

A particularly nasty spot called Spitwallys always tempted us. At certain water levels a great surf wave we just couldn't resist would form. If you missed your roll in this hole and had to bail out of your boat it could be tough to swim out of. On this day I ended up being trashed in Spitwallys. Tumbling over and over made catching my breath almost impossible. Lincoln knew the procedure for rescuing someone from a hole so he paddled his boat up from the downriver side of the hole and presented the nose of the boat so I could grab it as he paddled backwards and pulled me to safety. This was taking far too long. He was being careful; the danger is that of being pulled into the hole by the person being rescued and making the situation far worse. I was close to drowning when he manoeuvred his boat into position for the grab. Lincoln was the recipient of a great big bear hug when we finally got to shore.

From that . . . to this . . . from daring rescues to clinging to the dock in calm water. I wrap him in a towel and he retreats to a lawn chair on the beach. By the time we leave for home, shortly after dinner, I can see how exhausted he is. I might be making memories but not the kind I hoped for.

John has left his paddleboard for us to use and Lincoln wants to try it out. On our second day, I buckle him into his life jacket and he climbs aboard from water knee deep and immediately stands up, just a foot or two from the dock. I have visions of him losing his balance and falling against the dock. We all do. A chorus of anxious voices orders him to kneel down. He gives up in frustration, and I think we have killed his enthusiasm for the paddleboard.

On the third day, he tries again and clears the dock on his knees but can't seem to figure out how to use the paddle. He is trying to use the single-bladed paddleboard paddle the way he would use a double-bladed kayak paddle. The solution is obvious. We hand him a kayak paddle and assume that he will stay on his knees. He, however, stands up on the paddleboard but is forced by the shorter length of the kayak paddle into a crouching position that looks uncomfortable as well as unstable.

To my initial surprise and delight, I see that he finds his rhythm and is moving quickly out into the lake before angling the paddleboard, quite capably, to follow the shoreline. He grows smaller and more distant as we watch in astonishment. It is my turn to panic. I beg my sons-in-law to go after him.

"What should we do?" they ask as they scramble to launch the canoe.

I have no idea.

"Just stay with him," I say.

Lincoln paddles to a distant point of land and then, before the boys have been able to catch up to him, he turns and heads back to our dock. I hold a picture of him in my mind, his thin frame balancing on the paddleboard—the awkward, almost impossible position, his body bent double over a paddle that is too short and all wrong—and the sure, swift strokes that carry him to his chosen destination and back to us again. That picture of all we have lost and of all we have not, not yet, that small triumphant picture, makes me smile. It tells the truth of him.

When we purchased the condo in Revelstoke, in the fall of 2013, it was with the intention of a quick move. The following ten months have become ones of such confusion and traumatic change that I only leave town for necessary medical appointments, and the move is temporarily off the table. My worries about Lincoln's rapid descent into dementia are compounded by anxiety about my mother. I know my brother, his wife, and my sisters are taking good care of her but I miss her very much. I need to see her, to hug her, to tell her how much I love her. I know I cannot travel with Lincoln on my own, and he gets upset when I suggest that I might leave him in John's capable care and go without him. In July, John comes to the rescue and offers to drive Lincoln and me to Victoria. We will stay with my brother, Bill, and his wife, Maion. We are both excited at the thought of this little trip.

It is lovely to be on Vancouver Island, to see my mom, my brother and Maion, and, by happy chance, Christopher, my nephew. Bill and Maion provide wonderful care—meals and chauffeuring and laughter. I spend most of my two days there with my mom while Bill and Lincoln roam Victoria's beaches and nature parks. My mother wonders why we are not staying with her. I explain that her tiny place in an assisted living facility would just be too small for the three of us. I remind her many times that Lincoln has dementia.

"He needs space, Mom. And he enjoys Bill's company so much. You remember how it was with Dad . . ."

"Your dad was as easy as can be!"

I bite my tongue. My dad was a very good man, but he was never an easy one. Bill and I chuckle over how selective her memory has become.

Our visit is happily timed to coincide with Mom's ninety-third birthday. Bill and Maion host a small family party for her, and she basks in the love and attention. It is a good visit, far more relaxing than I could ever have imagined, thanks to Bill, Maion, and John.

On the drive home, Lincoln and I ride together in the back seat. When we stop in Osoyoos for a root beer, I suggest he move to the front in the hope that reclining the seat might make it easier for him to sleep. Soon, John and I both notice his speech getting clearer. He starts to question where we are going and the direction we are taking.

At this point in his illness, Lincoln struggles to express even the simplest ideas in words. When he does speak, his voice is quiet and hesitant. However, if he is upset, he becomes unusually articulate, sometimes using more sophisticated vocabulary than has ever been typical of him. This clear communication ought to be something to celebrate except that it forebodes, always, a crisis in his behaviour, usually marked by paranoia.

When I ask my neurologist about this, he suggests that as Lincoln's brain moves into fight-or-flight mode, the adrenalin and other neurotransmitters impact his speech centre, temporarily boosting his verbal performance. As soon as he starts suggesting that John is driving the wrong way, I realize I forgot to slip his medication into his juice at breakfast.

This is my fault! I think to myself.

"This is bullshit!" he says.

He hardly ever swears. My anxiety rises. So do his anger and frustration. No amount of reassurance works. When he undoes his seat belt, John immediately pulls over and gives him gentle hell before clipping him in again. I shift to the middle of the back seat so I can keep a firm hand over his seat belt's release button. As we climb Anarchist Mountain, an incredibly steep series of switchbacks on Highway 3, just east of Osoyoos, Lincoln opens his door. John whips us into the pullout, the big one that overlooks the town and the lake. Are there angels who can manipulate where these things happen?

We all get out. And there we are, the three of us, at the top of Anarchist, baking in the hot sun, looking down to the town and the lake, a glorious view that we are all too stressed to appreciate, and at an absolute impasse. I am reminded of the first time I ever drove this route and misread the sign.

"Antichrist Mountain!" I said at the time. "What kind of name is that?"

John and I try to persuade Lincoln to get into the back seat of the car, where at least the locks can be controlled, but Lincoln demands the key, insisting that he drive. Short of manhandling him into the car, action neither of us is willing to take, there is nothing to do but stay calm and wait it out.

Parkinson's disease affects the sympathetic nervous system that regulates body temperature. Most parkies have poor heat tolerance and I am no exception. I can feel the heat taking my legs out from under me. I tell John I am feeling unwell but that I have a plan. I'll call 911, not for me, but to resolve the situation. It seems extreme but so does leaving John alone, with one of us suffering from heat exhaustion and the other spiralling out of control. I make the call, explain the circumstances to the dispatcher, and suggest that the authoritative presence of a cop might help us all get back into the car. I tell her there is no need for sirens or an ambulance. I make no effort to hide what I am doing from Lincoln.

"He's not violent," I say. "He just won't get into the car. I think he will for a police officer."

She tells me she will send someone right away. We wait over fifteen minutes. I take refuge in the car and slip Lincoln's medication into his root beer. For reasons known only to him, Lincoln gets into the back seat beside me, and I hand him his drink. I call 911 and have the dispatch cancelled. He sips his root beer and begins to mellow out. From Rock Creek on, the familiar sequence of Midway, Greenwood, the Phoenix ski hill turnoff, and finally Grand Forks reassures him. Back at home, we are able to unpack and eat a little snack, all peacefully.

"I can't get over that young cop," he says, just before bed.

"What do you mean?" I ask him.

"Driving us all this way."

I can't know how he perceives the events at the top of Anarchist, but he knows it was a mess and, in the morning, asks me "not to tell." Now he is pacing and looking for his debit card, which I found for him last night and which he has stashed somewhere, but not in any of his usual hiding places. It must feel so out of control. It is obvious being away from home is not good for him, as episodes of paranoia, like this one and the one at the movie theatre, have followed out-of-town trips. There can't be another until we finally move to Revelstoke. I can't imagine how that will be. Or when it will be. I hope, by then, change won't affect him so.

It has never taken much to move me to tears. I am not alone. In our family we have two distinct groups: the stoics, my sister Margaret and my dad; and the weepers, my mother, my brother, my sister Jane, and me. My nephew Sam calls our family's tendency toward wet-eyed reactions "the Davidson blubber gene." For a few days, I am shaky and anxious and crying over the slightest trigger, from a sympathetic glance to a sad story on the news. I accept this as an appropriate reaction to all that has happened.

We will get back on track, I think.

Sleep and calm and home will work their mediating effect on both of us. I thank goodness for John. He and Mary Ann have created a beautiful backyard garden of flowers and vegetables, fruit trees, cobbled paths, and shady nooks. They have their youngest, and her two little ones, with them right now, and John says that his greatest pleasure is watching his grandkids follow each other through the garden and delight in the magic of his making. I am glad he has that. I know how upsetting the scene at the lookout was for him, too.

That night at the movie theatre, that morning at the river, the hot afternoon on Anarchist Mountain, and all the other times I have had to plead with Lincoln's illness to believe me, to see me as me, they are just moments. And fear? Fear, harsh and unavoidable, is just one way to be in the world. Sometimes I give it too much power, allowing it to displace hope and innumerable small joys. I think of Morocco and Monsieur le Maire and how afterward I played and replayed the awful thing that might have happened but didn't, and how Lincoln listened but couldn't understand my need to perseverate.

"Look where we are," he kept reminding me. "Look what we're doing."

I wasn't wrong to acknowledge my fears, and he wasn't wrong to turn his face toward what was real and beautiful and good.

I was frightened at the top of Anarchist but we got through it. I think about the young cop who never was, and our good friend John who is. We got through a lot of tricky situations but it was never easy. If there is a worry gene to partner that blubber gene, I am definitely a carrier.

"I want to go to Rilkoff's," he tells me one summer evening.

"Okay," I say. "We can do that."

Rilkoff's is a Grand Forks landmark, a large market and garden centre on the western end of town.

"What do you want to do there?" I ask him.

"Let's go!" he insists.

We get into the car, and at the end of our block I turn west onto Central Avenue, which becomes Highway 3.

"Where are you going?" he asks.

"To Rilkoff's, honey."

"This isn't the way!"

"It is, Lincoln. We'll be there in five minutes."

He continues to protest while I struggle to remain calm and reassuring. When we pull into the Rilkoff's parking lot, he wants to know why we are here.

"You said you wanted to come here and so I've brought us here."

"Not here! R-r-rilkoff's!"

"Buddy, look at the sign. The sign says Rilkoff's."

"Not here." He is close to tears. "Rilkoff's."

I don't know what he wants or how to help him.

"To Val and Terry's?" I ask.

Val and Terry Rilkoff were the original owners of the garden centre and still live in the valley. We see them every week at the farmers' market and picked cherries in their orchard earlier in the summer.

"No," he answers. "The other one."

"I don't know which other one you mean."

"Go that way," he says and points back to town.

As we approach our corner, I ask him if we are going home.

"No!"

"Keep going?"

"Yes."

He sits erect, tense and alert, peering out the windows into the growing dark, his head swivelling first to the windshield and then to the side window, back and forth, back and forth. We cross the bridge at the east end of town and I have to consider how far to go.

"I'm going to turn around at the Grand Forks sign," I tell him. "It's too dark. I don't want to hit a deer."

"Rilkoff's," he exhales, one last time. He sounds completely, utterly defeated.

Back at home, I park the car and run around to help him out. He can't manage the seat belt on his own or open the car door.

"I'm sorry," I say. "I know that wasn't what you wanted."

He doesn't utter another word as I help him into the house and get him ready for bed.

One day, several years later and after his death, I walk alone beside the Columbia River in Revelstoke and think of him on that bewildering, unhappy evening when we both tried so hard. In the way you suddenly recall a name you have been struggling to remember, I understand what he was trying to say, where he wanted to go. Not to Rilkoff's but to Revelstoke. I am sure of it.

Revelstoke.

To see his girls.

It is a sweet photograph I hold in my hand, taken by a friend of many years who is visiting from Vancouver. Her camera catches us in the early dusk of a summer evening, Lincoln and me, standing together at the road end of the old black trestle bridge that crosses the Kettle River just before it reaches City Park. The bridge is an iconic Grand Forks landmark, a gathering spot for local kids and a favourite launch pad for daredevil, into-the-river jumpers. Our after-dinner walkabouts often take us there. Lately he has been frightened on the bridge, reluctant to cross on his own but still willing to try if I take his hand.

In the photo we are both smiling, a little tentatively, and I am thin, thinner than I have ever been in my adult life. Lincoln has started to develop the physical parkinsonisms that mark the progression of Lewy body dementia, and the picture shows how stooped he is becoming. It cannot show how soft-spoken he is or the aphasia that steals his words. It doesn't tell of his frequent choking spells or his increased lack of balance or his shuffling gait. It does, however, reveal his gentleness and also his bewilderment. If I were to line it up, side by side, with any photo taken of him, even a year earlier, the differences would be almost unbearable to contemplate, his fearlessness becoming dependence and his cheerful intensity dissolving into a hesitant question.

We both look tired, and we are. Parkinson's alone messes with my sleep patterns and causes sudden, unpredictable episodes of exhaustion that I can only describe as having the rug pulled out from under me. He is up in the night for two to three hours, and so, of course, am I. His restless nights cause daytime weariness and he naps throughout the day, but by dinner we are both holding on as best we can until we go, mercifully, to bed.

The fatigue is exacerbating all my Parkinson's symptoms; I am shaky and lose my balance unexpectedly, but most troubling is that my medication is causing nausea to the point of vomiting, a symptom I experienced when I first started taking it two years previously. I know I need to eat more but I am scared to.

I hire help for our troubled nights. Marilyn is a dear friend. We met years earlier in the produce section of the grocery store. We both had tiny babies tied to our chests and delighted in the discovery that both babies were born at home. I taught her tiny baby when she came to kindergarten, and several of her siblings as well. A retired nurse, Marilyn is experienced working with dementia patients, and very kind. She comes every other night. Despite the respite she provides, I know I am not doing well. She encourages me to book an appointment with Molly, the home-to-care coordinator. I know where this is heading and am sick at the thought of it, but I make the call and ask Kathy to come with me.

"I need someone with a functioning brain there," I tell her.

Chris will stay with Lincoln.

Molly questions me about everything—my weight loss, how often I cry, and the details of the care I am providing for Lincoln. I tell her that he needs my help to dress and undress, to eat, to shower, and to use the toilet and that I am constantly dizzy from bending over and standing up, from tying shoes or taking them off, pulling up his pants, or helping him in and out of the car. She tells me that she never noticed my Parkinson's symptoms before but now they are obvious to her.

"I would like to fast-track him for placement," she says. "Either that or we are going to have to find beds for both of you."

He has no choice in the matter, and I tell myself I have no choice either. My rational brain agrees, but even as I type these words, I experience all over again the pain of that decision. Even though our friends and family are fully supportive, and I cannot imagine how I could have managed otherwise, still the question nags. If I were stronger or less selfish, more practical or less emotional, could I have kept him at home with me?

And I must tell our girls. I know they will understand—that is not a worry—but they love their dad very much. It is so hard for any of us to imagine he will be anything other than lost and desolate when he is placed in care.

My Sarah and Naomi,

I am so sorry I just can't keep on doing this for your dad. We haven't had much time to get used to how quickly this has progressed, have we? Molly says weeks, not months.

Each day seems to bring another change. Grocery shopping together has become almost impossible. Lincoln stops in the aisle and resists moving on. He isn't upset, just gone somewhere else. He is seldom sad . . . so confused . . . but not sad, not that I can tell, and so sweet to everyone who drops in.

Our backyard becomes a refuge for us both. Our crabapples are dropping, and it is an everyday chore keeping them cleaned up. I rake and Lincoln shovels them into boxes. We give some to a friend who has horses, and the rest he packs over to the compost bin. The neighbourhood deer push their noses through the fence and watch us as we work. I imagine I hear them telepathically calling to us.

Open the gate, they chant. *O-pen-the-gate.*

6 It Takes a Village

OUR FRIEND YVONNE runs the recreation program at Hardy View Lodge in Grand Forks, and once the decision is made to place Lincoln on the waiting list, she suggests he go to the day program held once a week for dementia patients. This will give him a chance to become familiar with his new home-to-be and maybe the break will be good for him. And good for me.

Anticipating Lincoln's reluctance to get on the bus for his first trip to "day camp," Yvonne drives the recreation department's bus right to our front door one afternoon after work. She takes Lincoln and me for a ride, a practice trip designed to ease his anxiety and mine. It works. He is excited to see her and climbs happily aboard.

Only in Grand Forks, I think to myself.

A day or two later, the local transit bus happens to stop near us while we are walking downtown. Lincoln immediately takes off toward it at a trot. The driver, Pierre, another friend and the husband of a teaching colleague, opens the door to greet him just as I catch up.

"We're not going on the bus today, buddy," I tell Lincoln.

"Another time, Lincoln," Pierre says. Then he adds, "You can have a ride any time you want."

I know things like this happen in other communities, but our kind, bus-driving friends make me very grateful for my small town. Every day—no matter how bleak—every day seems to have its measure of goodness. Every day has its gold.

Kathy and I meet with Cynthia, the lovely woman who is the patient care coordinator at Hardy View Lodge. As we tour the facility, we work out a strategy for transitioning Lincoln into care. Hardy View is divided into five "cottages," separate units of about a dozen individual rooms arranged around an attractive communal space that is both lounge and dining area. It is clean, modern, full of sunlight, and decorated with artwork and quilts on the wall. As we tour, I am greeted by staff members who are friends, or parents of kids we've taught, or the kids themselves, all grown up and working now as care aides and nurses, cleaners and clerks.

"We'll take good care of him," I hear over and over.

I know they will. He is a well-loved man, and these are good people, but I cannot stop myself from quietly weeping the entire time.

We decide that when his room becomes available, he will go to the day program and then be taken by staff members through the corridors and into the residential wing to his room. While he is in the day program, a few friends and I will get his room ready. I make lists of the things I need to provide and consider what to bring from home: his favourite chair, a small table, and a CD player, poster-sized photographs of Lincoln on mountaintops, holding rattlesnakes, snowboarding, and skydiving. I want his new caregivers to have a sense of who he was before dementia, to be able to see in this frail, quiet, old man the vibrant, energetic force of nature that was my husband. I hope Lincoln will look at the pictures and see himself not with regret for what he has lost but with pride and delight in his life well lived. And there are other pictures, too, of Lincoln and me, of Lincoln and the Lost Boys, and of our girls and their families.

All this planning is a diversion, but not diversion enough. I knew it would be hard, but I had no idea how hard. I am two people, one capable and proactive and the other distraught and fearful. While anticipating the change to come, I feel myself possessed, as if my emotions were manifesting as beings separate from the me-who-used-to-be. Grief lives in my chest and rises in my throat. It spills out of my eyes unbidden and unannounced. Insistent and intrusive, it cannot be ignored. But it is a simple emotion, a sharp, clean pain, and understandable, unlike the guilt that lives in my belly, stealing my appetite and haunting my sleep, a goblin, contrary and confusing. A conundrum. I make myself crazy with wondering if I would feel even worse if I didn't feel so intensely guilty. Is my guilt somehow a good thing, a measure of my goodness as a person? I mean, a good person wouldn't do this easily, would they? A good person would feel guilty.

But then, of course, the goblin says, *a good person would not do this at all.*

And the relief? Where shall I stash that? It is a secret I can scarcely bear to admit to myself, much less to anyone else. But I am relieved. I know others are because they tell me so. I try to take it as an intended kindness when people tell me how necessary this is, how wise, but it makes me irrationally angry that no one is on his side. No one questions my decision. I need the support, but for his sake, part of me would like to be challenged.

They're worried about you, I tell myself. *They know you're struggling. If someone else were in this situation, you would understand. Wouldn't you?*

I seek advice in all the ways I know—from the excellent therapist Lincoln and I visited during a troubled time in our marriage, from our family and closest friends, from the Alzheimer Society of British Columbia, and from the family support workers attached to Hardy View.

They all counsel patience and offer reassurance and practical suggestions. They tell me that when the time comes, it will be difficult but doable. They tell me I am strong and that Lincoln knows how much I love him. I nod and smile and agree, but when I am alone I question everything. I don't feel strong. And how will he know I love him? What will happen to us?

A friend who was coming two mornings a week to take Lincoln for walks is no longer comfortable with the level of intimate care required. I understand. She was away on holiday for a month and came home to find him very changed. It has been hard for her.

I do get out thanks to Chris and John, who say they can handle whatever comes their way in terms of care. One or the other stays with Lincoln when I make my weekly visit to my personal trainer. She makes me sweat and follows up with a pep talk and a hug.

I suspect conversations have been taking place about feeding us. One friend drops off borshch for our dinner and another calls to say she will be delivering dinner tomorrow. It is a huge help and one of the benefits of having lived in the same small town for thirty-four years. The learning here is all about accepting help. It is much harder than I imagined. I am acutely uncomfortable being on the receiving end of attention and concern and, at the same time, overwhelmed by the goodness of the people in our lives. One part of me is mourning, one part thankful, and one part wondering how I can possibly repay all this kindness.

Hi John,

Daycare today seems to have gone okay. I stayed for about twenty minutes and left him sitting around the table with the two other Tuesday clients, sipping mint tea with honey. Bingo was not a hit but he apparently enjoyed the rock collection they handed him. He fell fast asleep within moments of getting home and stayed that way for an hour. There wasn't any sign of increased upset, though when he woke up he thought he might just go home for a quick visit.

He had a "visit" from Christine, his sister, in the night and it made him sad. I told him she was just saying hello and letting him know she was okay and had found their mom and dad. He remembered it this morning. It might come up. He also confuses my name with "Elizabeth." That sometimes comes out when he wants to say "Leslie." I like being the Queen.

When we moved to Grand Forks in the summer of 1981, our first home was a little white frame heritage house on Central Avenue, complete with a picket fence and a wraparound front veranda. "Heritage" in Grand Forks usually means "charming on the outside, needs a lot of work on the inside." Our little house fit those criteria perfectly.

The kitchen floor was aslant; it felt a bit like walking into a funhouse until we got used to it. Crumbs, dirt, and dust bunnies tended to migrate into one corner. There was no heat upstairs except for what was provided by a small baseboard heater in the bathroom. Everything was old and worn, from the vinyl flooring to the bathroom fixtures, and we loved it. It took every penny of our savings as well as loans from our parents to make the down payment. We'd landed jobs in the same school; Lincoln worked afternoons as the teacher-librarian and I worked mornings teaching kindergarten, a perfect arrangement of sharing the work and sharing the parenting of Sarah, then eleven months old.

We could not believe our luck in all things Grand Forks, the friendliness of the people, the beauty in the landscape. Happy Valley, I named it then. In the six years we'd been together, we'd lived longer in our Volkswagen Westfalia than in any other place, but we were home now, in our little house, and we knew it.

Four years to the day after our arrival, Naomi was born in the upstairs bedroom and now we were four. As the kids grew, the house seemed to shrink. One Friday evening, Lincoln and I found ourselves sitting in our bedroom upstairs, trying to read and escape the gang of young teens who had colonized our downstairs.

"I think we need more room," I said. "Maybe it's time to move."

Lincoln winced. He was perfectly happy where we were, but he liked the house I found for us just one block east and around the corner. Another old fixer-upper. It was an odd choice, I know, for two people with no fixer-upper-ing skills but it sat on three lots on Eighth Street and was well off busy Central Avenue. There was a front veranda, a screened-in back porch, fruit trees, gardens galore, and a double carport attached to a separate shed. There was one more bedroom than we had before, a big kitchen, a sunlit dining room, and a funky, semi-finished basement that came with a pool table. A place for the girls and their friends! No more Friday nights spent banished to our bedroom. I loved the new house for its high ceilings and bay windows, for its beautiful gardens and pine trees and lilacs, for the peace and quiet of the backyard, even for the deer that cost us a fortune in fencing but slept through the winter nights beneath our maple tree and hid their babies among the shrubs below the dining room windows each spring.

But a garden can't comfort you if you have no time to enjoy it. Lilac trees won't put out your garbage or bring soup to your door when you are on your third sleepless night in a row. And high ceilings don't watch out for your husband or take him for walks or keep him safe.

I cry more times than I can count on our neighbour Lee's shoulder. Sometimes she cries, too, but wallowing is not in her emotional vocabulary so I try to eliminate it from mine.

Barb and Steve live in the house beside us. Barb, a master gardener, helps me simplify my outdoor chores. She offers not only advice but also hours, no, days of labour. Steve builds fences and gates and mulches our leaves. And they both come at a moment's notice if I need to call for help.

One morning Lincoln can't find his hat. He is sure Steve has it. "He's got one just the same!" Lincoln argues, forcefully and articulately, an indication he is upset and possibly heading for an episode of paranoia.

He marches next door to demand the hat's return, and Steve and Barb both calmly and cheerfully go through the charade of searching for the hat. Steve even offers to lend him one. That kindness takes the wind out of the paranoia boat's sails and Lincoln lets me take him home.

Later that day I find the hat in one of his backpacks, not the one he normally uses. I have no idea how, or why, he put it there.

He is having an agitated day. He hasn't had one for a long time. We go for mail and I have to abort the grocery-buying mission. That can wait for another day, but I really need some juice for dinner so I can get his meds into him. I email Barb to tell her we found the hat and ask her to buy the juice. In the meantime, I make a pot of herbal tea and stir a few drops of his medication into his cup along with the honey.

I hardly know the two young women who move in down the street. We've had brief conversations but I have no idea what they understand of our circumstances. One day, we are both outside doing yard work in the backyard. I am on my hands and knees, weeding and deadheading flowers. Large ponderosa pines border the back of our property, and Lincoln is picking up the prickly pine cones in the yard with one of those trigger-handled trash-grabber sticks. It's a never-ending task and I assume he will be busy with it for a while. When I notice he isn't in the yard, my heart stops. I fly into the house, hoping to find him rooting in the fridge for a snack or in the bathroom, but he isn't. Nor is he in the shed or in Barb and Steve's backyard. Gone! I've lost him! I run to the front of the house and look one way down our street and then the other. I spot him at the end of the block, talking to one of the young women, and hurry to join them.

"Lincoln tells me he's going for a walk," she says. "I was just suggesting that I could go with him."

"It's okay," I tell her. "I could use a walk, too." I whisper, "Thank you."

"We're here if you need us," she says, this kind almost-stranger. "Any time."

I know she means it. Everyone on the block looks out for him. Everyone offers help.

"Day or night," they say.

———————

I have done the unthinkable and Lincoln now lives in Hardy View Lodge. The move goes as planned, and I guess, as far as these things go, it goes well. I don't recall it clearly. I do remember that the staff are kind and patient despite the challenges they face with him. Like many dementia sufferers, he doesn't know to stop when dressing or undressing himself. He piles on three or four T-shirts or strips naked. He wanders the cottage and tries all the exit doors. He wanders into the rooms of other residents, most of whom are women, older than he is, and very frail. Sometimes a staff member greets me with a complaint about his behaviour when I arrive at the cottage to visit.

"If he were easy, he wouldn't be here," I am tempted to say but I bite my tongue. I see how hard they work, how much they care.

At first, he is devastated, utterly bewildered. His sense of abandonment is profound.

"No one wants me," he tells me over and over.

"I want you," I say. "I love you."

My words bring him no comfort. How could they?

"Did I do something wrong?" he asks me.

"Oh, sweetheart, no. No."

I visit him for lunch and dinner. I sit with him at the table we share with a sweet, middle-aged man. I take him outside for long walks or to sit in the sun in the garden. After every visit, I must wait in the car, in the parking lot, until I can stop crying for long enough to drive home.

Then he is angry with me. He ignores me or treats me coldly when I visit. I find myself wishing he would forget who I was so I could be the one who has the right to feel hurt. That might be better than this horrible guilt. I keep visiting and stick to my two-hours-twice-a-day schedule, and if he is unresponsive, I engage with the other residents. During mealtimes I chat with our table-mate or help others with their food. After dinner, if he won't walk with me, I do simple puzzles with a couple of the women. I sing "You Are My Sunshine" with an old dear who knows all the verses. The rest of the time she sings only in Russian. Slowly I become more comfortable in the cottage, and slowly Lincoln either for-gives or forgets the role I played in his displacement.

"Lincoln, who is this?" one of the care aides asks one day as I bend over to kiss him hello.

"My one and only," he says.

Another day he greets me with surprise.

"They let you out!"

He packs his clothes in the bags that line his garbage can. I will see this again and again in other new residents, and I will never get used to the heartbreak of it. How unhappy they must be, separated from all that is familiar at a time in their lives when they are least able to understand why.

"Lincoln, we are happy to have you here," the nurse tells him.

"Happy to be here," he replies without missing a beat. Ever a gentleman.

The first month in care passes and now his face lights up each time I arrive. I realize that, released from the burden of care and the constant vigilance, I am healthier, stronger, and calmer, though I feel huge guilt that my recovery comes at such cost to him. Our time together is tender and loving, and I no longer sob in the car at the end of each visit.

I hear from the staff that he still roams the common room at night after I have left, piling furniture and trying to climb it. I wonder if he is attempting to escape or if my mountain man simply needs to climb something, anything.

And my nights alone are hard. Sometimes I frighten myself with the intensity of my sorrow. It cracks me wide open and it hurts like nothing I have ever experienced. I close the windows of our house, even on the milder autumn nights, for fear my sobbing will be overheard. It feels as if this grief comes from someone else, somewhere else. But it is me making this noise, and I wonder if it will ever stop. And despite my knowledge of all the dreadful woes of this world, I am dying of self-pity.

When my sister Jane suggests I watch a CBC television interview with the author and former broadcaster Louise Penny, I hesitate. I am a fan of Louise Penny and her Three Pines mystery novels. I have recently learned that her husband lives with dementia, and I am cautious about having to bear witness to another's pain. I also worry about being confronted with a model of someone "doing it better"—being more accepting or showing more courage. I don't want my nose rubbed in my own inadequacy.

I do watch, and in the wondrous way of things unfolding as they should, I find the interview helpful and comforting. Louise speaks about the gift of the "long goodbye," of her gratitude that she and her husband, Michael, have been able to say what they needed to say to each other, that what is left for them to experience is stripped to its essence. Love is what remains.

She speaks, too, of the support she and Michael receive from others, and I recognize something of our experience, mine and Lincoln's, in theirs. Until now, I have seen our "long goodbye" only as excruciating pain, but now I think of all the opportunities we are being given, the sweet and tender moments, the honest, loving conversations we've had, and the laughter. I think of our girls and the good men they've married, how often they travel to see us, and how much they love their father. They bring their babies, and he drinks them in with his eyes and embraces them with his smile. A demon is banished as a result of watching that interview and, as it turns out, remains in exile. When everything else is stripped away, love is what remains.

———————

I arrive before dinner one evening to find Lincoln piling the dining room chairs onto the tables while a frustrated staff member tries to place dishes for dinner. There is something very familiar in what he is doing but it takes me a while to make the connection. Then I see it: Lincoln in his library at Hutton School, where he taught for thirty years, lifting chairs onto the tables at the end of the day.

"Hey, buddy," I say. "Fred isn't going to be cleaning the floor tonight. You don't have to stack the chairs."

"Okay," he says happily, and I lead him away for a stroll.

———————

My Dear Sibs,

He had a physio assessment done today and our friend Margo will be the physio assistant providing the hands-on therapy. She is a bulldog when it comes to her patients but has been off since the spring with a broken ankle. I will be glad to have her in our corner. Tomorrow the occupational therapist comes to talk wheelchairs and/or walkers. I can't take him for a walk in the building by myself without having something for him to lean on or sit on. When he tires, it is exactly as if someone pulled his plug.

He is very bent over and today I found him asleep in his arm-chair with his head on his knees. They are talking about a reclining wheelchair for his tired times. I found a spare wheelchair to use while we wait to get his ordered.

Yesterday was very, very hard and today he and I even laughed together, probably not at the same thing, but at the same time, and he felt more relaxed. So that's good.

I am eating as well as I can manage, slowly catching up on sleep, trying to figure out a daily routine of sorts. Lincoln has me and some truly wonderful friends paying attention to, and for, him, so please don't worry about us. I will holler if the centre feels like it's not going to hold. Love you all very much,

L

The cyclist pedalling toward us looks so much like Lincoln that I stop in my tracks. Beside me, Leora sighs a soft "oh" and touches my arm. She sees it, too. We are walking the abandoned railbed pathway that runs above the Granby River, a long beautiful stretch of the Trans Canada Trail just outside of Grand Forks city limits. Tears instantly blur my vision. I hate that I can't control them. I've struggled to manage that damn blubber gene all my life, but it kicks into overdrive with a relentless vengeance the day Lincoln takes up residence in Hardy View Lodge.

The man on the bike is wearing a hat just like Lincoln's. His sunglasses, his grey-white beard, and even his posture over the handlebars are all achingly familiar. He comes closer and I recognize a face I love, but I am surprised to have confused it with Lincoln's. It's our dear friend Chris, and until that moment, I would never have thought it possible to see one in the other, to mistake, even for a second, Kathy's stocky, blond-haired and blue-eyed Christopher for my skinny, dark-haired, brown-eyed husband.

How did this happen? I think. *When did it happen?*

We've all seen the photographs of dogs and their owners who resemble each other—or of elderly couples who have grown physically alike as they age. Do old friends do the same thing?

There is a photograph of Lincoln and Chris framed and hanging on my kitchen wall. Chris is pushing Lincoln in the wheelchair against a backdrop of golden-leaved fall trees. Again, they are wearing the same hat, the same sunglasses, sporting identical beards, and beaming the same happy grin toward the camera, and yes, they look uncannily alike. The photo must have been taken before the day that Leora and I met Chris on the trail, because when I tell Kathy about that moment of confusion and how it made me cry, she insists that Chris put away the hat and buy himself a new one, in a different colour.

We've known Kathy and Chris almost as long as we have lived in Grand Forks. We are all teachers. Kathy and I shared a kindergarten classroom for several years until we got pregnant just months apart. Kindergarten was a half-day program, and when Naomi was two years old, Lincoln's library assignment increased to full-time and we needed daycare. While Kath taught the morning class, I cared for both toddlers, Chris and Kathy's Ian and our Naomi. In the afternoons, while I taught, Kath did the same.

Kathy and Chris taught our girls how to ride a two-wheeler, how to get on and stay on the T-bar at the ski hill, and, eventually, how to drive. They graciously handled Naomi puking all over the back seat of their new car on the way to Big White ski hill and didn't freak out when Naomi and Ian filled their hot tub with Oregon grape berries to make the water look like blood.

Every Christmas Eve, both families gathered at our house. Fuelled by shortbread, butter tarts, and Nanaimo bars, we read Christmas stories aloud and banged and clanged away on rhythm instruments to accompany the singing of Christmas carols. At some point in the evening, Lincoln and Ian, the two quiet souls in our noisy group, would sneak off to the relative peace of the basement and play pool. Christmas dinner was spent at Kathy and Chris's house, followed by board games. As the kids grew up, the circle expanded to include their romantic partners. Our last Christmas together included a couple of tiny grandchildren. We all still maintain the traditions, though we can no longer be together.

We took our last trip to Mexico with Kathy and Chris. Our last ski weekend was in their company, as was our last camping trip, our last long bike ride, our last kayak paddle.

Now, with Lincoln in care, one or both of them visit almost daily. Kathy keeps him supplied with homemade cookies and muffins. They invite me to dinner several times a week, and when Kathy is away attending to her mom in Kelowna, she leaves orders with Chris to take me out to dinner and feed me.

Kathy doesn't have a blubber gene. She is very kind and very practical. I learned early in our relationship that her stoicism does not mean she lacks empathy. Her heart is large and it breaks as easily as anyone's, but grief will never derail her or stop her from doing what needs to be done. I am grateful she takes my tendency to bawl in her stride, that she doesn't see it as a sign of weakness.

Kathy and I have not grown into physical similarity as our husbands have. No one will mistake one of us for the other. We've walked hundreds—maybe thousands—of kilometres together and shared hundreds—maybe thousands—of bottles of wine, but even mosquitoes know we are different. Kathy doesn't need to wear repellent when she walks with me. I take all the bites for both of us.

We don't look alike but we do finish each other's sentences. We speak the same languages, "grandmother-ese" and "teacher-talk." Kath is still working as a teacher on call and I live vicariously through her stories.

Perhaps, some future day, two friends will walk a route so familiar to Kathy and me—up Goat Mountain Road and along the Trans Canada Trail to the lookout. As they stop to take in the scene that spreads out below, river and meadow and rising hills, two bearded old men wearing identical hats will cycle past. Moments later, heard before they are seen, two aging women, one flapping at mosquitoes, will drift by in a haze of conversation and laughter.

"Old friends," one of the walkers will say as the women disappear around the next bend.

"Yes," the other will reply.

"Old friends."

7 *Ducks in a Row?*

WITH LINCOLN NOW LIVING IN Hardy View Lodge, two things must happen before I can move forward with our plan to move to Revelstoke. I must sell the Grand Forks house and Lincoln must be transferred to Mount Cartier Court, Revelstoke's long-term care facility. The timing is going to be everything.

In January 2015, I request his placement on the waiting list in Revelstoke and am told it will take six to eight months before a room will be available for him.

Spring at the earliest, I think. *Fall at the latest.*

I set to work preparing the house for the move. I begin with the little building at the end of our driveway. It's not a garage but more of a shed or shop, complete with a workbench and an ancient wood-burning stove. It has been a catch-all for our active family's outdoor stuff—gardening implements, sports equipment, wood-working tools, and camping gear, all in multiples because Lincoln never threw away anything. When a ski pole broke he kept its partner, "just in case." In with a new bike did not mean out with an old. Ever. The same applied to skis, snowboards, backpacks, snowshoes, kayaks, paddles, wetsuits, life jackets, camping gear, tarpaulins, chains, rope, lawn chairs, air mattresses, tennis rac-quets, bocce balls, croquet mallets, and hockey sticks. Lincoln never met a bungee cord he didn't love or a broken tool that he could bear to toss. In my husband's world, duct tape fixed every-thing. But some things are not fixable, and Lincoln has no idea that his shed is being readied for the stuff of another family's life. Though I have long grumbled about the state of that shed, I find the act of culling its thirty-four years' worth of accumulated contents incredibly difficult.

"Lincoln would be so upset if he could see all this being given away," I tell the wise therapist I now see several times a month. "I feel so guilty."

I expect her response to be empathetic and reassuring. She is that kind of person. However, she does not say, "He would understand" or, "This must be very difficult for you."

"Hmm," she muses. "What do you think guilt is?"

I don't know how to respond. She rephrases her question.

"You say it makes you feel guilty to have cleaned out the shed. I wonder how you define guilt? That's all."

After thinking about it for a moment, I tell her I think guilt is an emotion experienced when we have wronged another and know it. It is what my mother would have called "your conscience talking."

She then wonders aloud if guilt serves a purpose. I suggest that if it leads to a sincere apology and an attempt to make the situation right, followed by a heartfelt commitment not to repeat the action, it is useful.

"It's a simple drill," I tell her. "If you screw up, say you're sorry and mean it. Then, try to fix it and don't do it again."

"And so why is it wrong to be clearing out the shed?" she asks. My turn to "hmm."

As a caregiver, I have been, by my own definition, guilty of any number of things, mostly impatience. Wrapped up in my own despair, I know I fail to understand the devastating effects of Lincoln's dementia on his ability to feel safe or at ease in the world. It is his grace and patience that teach me hard lessons about compassion and acceptance. The Parkinson's beast has had lessons for me, too. I fed it on stress and fatigue and it grew quickly. I started vomiting up my meds and was too weary to exercise.

I looked in the mirror and could not recognize the haggard old woman looking back at me. I shook and wobbled and made the good people in our lives anxious on my behalf. If I wanted to be the caregiver that Lincoln deserved, I needed to be strong and healthy, resilient. I needed to ask for help. And so I did. Guilt had served its purpose.

"What if they find a cure for Lewy body dementia tomorrow," I say, "and I get to bring Lincoln home? What is he going to do when he sees what I have done to his shed?"

It is an image both joyous and cringeworthy. It makes us laugh, the kind of laughter that lives one breath away from tears. I am not going to be bringing Lincoln home, but my feelings about the culling of the shed do not seem to fit my notion of guilt. There will be no easily recited "drill" for getting through this. I tell myself it is just stuff in that shed, possessions, objects, all replaceable, but it is stuff that speaks about our whole family. It is stuff that represents how enriched my life and our children's lives have been because of Lincoln's passion for the outdoors and his eagerness to share it with the people he loves. It is the stuff of our memories.

Cleaning out the shed, even with the help of our supportive tribe of friends, means that I am now on my own, alone in a way I have never been before, responsible for every decision affecting us both. Even though I have been "the boss of us" for a long time, I still share my thoughts with him and look for signs of his approval. I have always had his thoughts or feelings to consider. Now I am forced into an independence I never wanted and if I am honest, it frightens me. Feeling guilty may be a whole lot easier than plumbing the depths of sadness that clearing out the stuff of our lives evokes in me. Feeling guilty may mean I do not have to acknowledge the many joys of my life, when all I want to do is weep.

"You have to look after yourself!"

I hear that once a week, if not more. I know the truth of that assertion. I get that it comes from a place of kindness and caring. But sometimes it makes me want to explode.

"Don't you think I know that?" I want to shout. "Why do you think my husband is in a long-term care facility? He's there so I can look after myself! Do you have any idea how that feels? Please don't tell me what to do."

How can anyone else know, for me, where necessary self-care ends and selfishness begins, when I hardly know it for myself? My therapist has spoken with many caregivers. She tells me I am not alone in my frustration and confusion. She knows how consuming a misplaced sense of guilt can be when we fail to manage the unmanageable. She understands how disloyal we feel when making the hard decisions, hopefully in our loved one's best interests, and our own. She tells me we are all trying to figure out how to tease out, from a huge tangle of emotions, the ones that are best to guide us, the ones that will hold us together as our worlds shift and crack. Empathy and reassurance. She is that kind of person. And we agree that guilt has its place in our emotional lives but it is a place we can too easily find. If we permit guilt to suspend our experience of our most profound pain, do we also allow it to diminish our capacity for joy?

And so I don't shout. I smile and carry on. I thank people for their kindness. It isn't courage, nor is it a lie. I am the only face of the twosome that once was Lincoln and Leslie—before Parkinson's, before dementia—that most people ever see now. I try to understand their concern for me as concern for us both. Our lives have changed and people care. That's what "Look after yourself" implies.

No, they don't know what I am going through, any more than I am privy to the hard truths of their lives. And so I don't shout. I dig into that tangle of emotion and I find, along with the anger and the regret, the grief and the guilt, a bright thread of gratitude. I cling to that. I have that choice.

Dear Robbin,

It is cloudy and cool this morning but Linc needs to get out so I will take warm clothes to him and see if we can manage a trip round the block with the walker.

One of the staff has a snake phobia. I have removed all the snake pics from his room. Poor woman, she was so nervous about talking to me about it. It must be an awful fear. I gave her a hug and got the pictures out of there. Funny old world.

Love,

L

Hi John,

Tomorrow is my birthday and Mel has invited Leora and me to the lake for coffee in the morning. Would it be possible for you to visit Lincoln tomorrow morning? I will give him lots of time today. If not, no problem.

Thanks,

L

Leslie,

Believe it or not we hadn't forgotten that it is your birthday tomorrow. Unless you want him all to yourself today (which is of course fine) I was planning to visit both days but maybe for longer tomorrow. Just a reminder that I am not doing this to be a nice guy and to help you and help Linc . . . I need to do this . . . part of my own grieving and it is good for me, even if sometimes tough.

John

PS: Do you know if you can get Wi-Fi up there?

Hi John,

I do understand the need to do this. I feel it and inwardly "prickle" when I get wise counsel to watch how much time I spend there.

And as for thinking you're a nice guy . . . puhleeze!

And yes, easy Wi-Fi.

L

NOT YET READY FOR THE OLD VOLKS' HOME

I am an attractive, silver-grey 1991 German who has been in two loving relationships that ended through no fault of mine. I don't drink oil to excess and am accident-free . . .

I prepare an online ad for the sale of the Volkswagen camper. This one, third in the line of our beloved Westies, is the one we bought as empty nesters. We call it the Silver Bullet, just for fun, because it is, like all Westfalias, a slow-moving box on wheels. It has to be sold, though it breaks my heart, because my misbehaving left foot means I can no longer drive a stick shift.

I go no further before I am hijacked by memory. That happens a lot these days.

1977. Lincoln and I are in Germany, taking possession of a brand new green Volkswagen Westfalia. We live in the van for over fifteen months while we travel through Europe and Morocco before, road weary and broke, we return home to Canada. The vw comes with us, and after visiting my parents in Ottawa, we head west in late November. We start handing out resumés when we hit the bc border and are in the Fort St. John school board office for less than an hour before we walk out with assignments that carry us through to June. Though the Peace River country is very beautiful and we make good friends quickly, it is also far from our West Coast family and the winters are long and harsh. We leave at the end of the school year and live in the Westie for the summer before moving into a rented oceanfront cottage near Gibsons, BC, on the Sunshine Coast. We marry in October of that year, and the following September finds us living, with our new baby girl, in family housing on the University of British Columbia campus. Lincoln completes a post-degree diploma program in school library science that leads to job offers for both of us at John A. Hutton Elementary School in Grand Forks.

The summer that Sarah is six and Naomi almost two, we plan a road trip to Inuvik, where my brother, Bill, and his family are living. We travel, of course, in the Westie and are thrilled to be on the road again. We wind our way up the Fraser Canyon, then through the Cariboo country before making a dinner stop in Prince George. We have been advised to carry extra gasoline on the long trek up the Dempster Highway, and we fill two jerry cans with fuel and fasten them onto the roof of the van. I am sitting in the back seat with Naomi, who is cranky after a long day confined to a car seat. Sarah is in front with her dad. We've just finished an on-the-go supper of sandwiches and apple slices. The landscape has been unchanging for a while. Trees, trees, and more trees. Just outside of Hudson's Hope, on a deserted section of the Alaska Highway connector, we startle to the sound of a loud bang from somewhere in the back of the van.

A tire, I think and brace for the swerving, wild ride that inevitably follows a rear tire blowout.

There is no swerving. No wild ride.

"What's going on?"

"We just lost power," Lincoln says and steers us to the side of the road. The van coasts to a stop.

The engine is situated in the rear of the vehicle, and I turn my head to look out the back window. I am bemused by the impossibility of the phenomenon unfolding on the other side of the glass, and it takes a few seconds for me to process what I am seeing— clouds of grey smoke billowing upward just outside the window.

"What the . . ."

Then flames, bright orange and growing quickly, answer my question.

"We're on fire!" I shout.

I fumble with my seat belt and then the straps of Naomi's car seat. Lincoln reaches over to unbuckle Sarah. With Naomi in my arms, I yank down on the handle of the sliding side door and slam it open. I jump from the van, my little one clutched to my chest. Lincoln races around the front of the vw and grabs Sarah. We pack our children well away from the now blazing camper. Then Lincoln races back to the vw and rifles through the front of the vehicle, pulling documents from the glove compartment and rescuing his beloved camera.

"Leave it!" I beg. "Please come away! Lincoln! The gasoline on the roof!"

"It'll burn," he hollers. "It won't explode. Full cans won't explode."

We are alone on a deserted section of a northern highway while the early summer sun sinks into dusk. Van flambé, served with a side of sobbing children and bordering-on-hysterical mother.

"I don't want to do this all by myself!" I wail. "Please, Lincoln!"

He finally joins us on the roadside as our dreams of an Arctic adventure are consumed by flames and belched out in clouds of black smoke. Then, while we watch, stunned and helpless, the van starts to roll along the gravel shoulder, slowly picking up speed on the downhill slope. Lincoln takes out his camera and clicks away.

"Guess the brake line just burned through," he says quietly. Click! Click!

Flames and smoke stream behind our Westie. Click! Then it comes to rest against one of the two huge, lacquered cedar logs that support a large sign. "Welcome to Hudson's Hope," it reads. The sign is very new, very shiny. It even has a protective awning constructed of cedar shakes.

Click! again while hungry tongues of fire lick at the varnished posts and the gleaming surface of the sign and reach greedily for the shake roof. There are now enough flames and smoke to attract attention, and the Hudson's Hope volunteer fire department screams its way toward us. They are not able to save the vehicle or the sign, but no one is hurt and we haven't started a forest fire. In the way of rural communities, kind strangers gather us up and take us in for the night before delivering us the next day to friends, Dawn and Jack, who live at Charlie Lake.

Despite my protests that there will be nothing left worth saving, Lincoln insists on one last visit to our Westie. I worry the sight of his beloved vehicle, utterly destroyed, along with all our belongings, meticulously packed by him over days and days, might be unnecessarily painful. A photograph shows what is left of the van, its apocalyptic-looking carcass, black and charred, and inside, wearing borrowed coveralls, a ruefully smiling Lincoln, crouching in what used to be the opening to the side door. Minutes after I have snapped the picture, he emerges and triumphantly presents me with our set of nesting cooking pots, unscathed by their trial by fire.

"Look at this!" he crows. "Isn't that amazing! Just look at this!"

"Yes! Amazing!" I tell him.

You're amazing, I think. *Does nothing bring you down?*

Our girls have the holiday of a lifetime on our kind friends' beautiful ranch at Charlie Lake, riding tractors, making campfires, and running free with Dawn and Jack's little boys. If the night of the fire caused any trauma, this idyllic week is, for them, the perfect therapy. Lincoln and I deal with insurance issues, shop for necessities, and plan the next steps.

We take the Greyhound to Prince George, where we board the BC Rail passenger train to North Vancouver. The trip along the Fraser River is thrilling to the point of hair-raising in the places where the train seems to cling, unsupported, to the side of the Fraser Canyon and the river churns and foams far, far below. The girls love the freedom to move about that the train provides. This is the way to travel with kids—no car seats, a bathroom always available, and a small canteen at the ready. We eat snacks and tell stories and wonder about the lives of the people we see in the tiny communities through which we pass. This is a very happy trip despite the circumstances that caused it.

Lincoln's mom and dad pick us up at the train station in North Vancouver and take us home with them to Abbotsford. We begin immediately to search for a second-hand car. We've talked at length about what we'd like. Something practical. A little Toyota Tercel, perhaps? Four-wheel drive would be great.

We both spot it the moment we pull into the dealership. It takes our breath away to see it there, our dear green Westie, reborn and waiting for us as if by magic. It is perfect and pristine, the identical model in every way, except it has a fraction of the van flambé's mileage. We are instantly smitten—and a salesman's dream. Never mind the unexplained exploding engine; never mind the lawsuit launched by the town of Hudson's Hope for the replacement of their sign; never mind the Westie's frigid interior in the winter or its suffocating heat in the summer; never mind how slowly it putt-putts up hills or how often we have to pull over to let lines of traffic pass us; never mind practical. This is the van of our hearts, of our wonderful wandering years, and our children are still small enough that it accommodates all four of us. But we can't really afford it.

"Never mind. We can make it work," Lincoln says. "Besides," he adds with a grin, "I saved the pots."

I watch the documentary *Alive Inside: A Story of Music and Memory*, a bittersweet portrayal of the impact music has on the lives of dementia patients. It shows how playing the music that brought them pleasure in the past profoundly affects their present existence. Lincoln has always had a CD player in his room, but after watching the movie, I go one step further and purchase a little iPod Shuffle and load it with his favourites. Leora knits a tiny pouch to hold it, for those times when he doesn't have a convenient pocket. This means he can have music anywhere, especially on those grim winter days when we can't go outside and have to walk the hallways instead. I don't see the dramatic results that are highlighted in the film, but I know it calms him, "lightens" him. Because he is deaf in his left ear, I often sit with him in the day room with the other earphone in my ear and we listen together. I must take the iPod with me each time I leave. I know it would not survive his constant reorganizing of his belongings.

His new wheelchair has arrived. It holds him in with good support and can be deeply reclined. He can rest comfortably as it also allows him to be positioned to compensate for the progressive curvature of his spine.

One day I go in at lunchtime, as always. I find him sitting on his bed, head down, as always. I kneel on the floor in front of him and arch my neck so he can see my face.

"Hi," I say as I slip the pouch with the iPod over his head.

He opens his eyes and stretches out his hand, placing it on my cheek, then leans forward to kiss me. It is the first time in many months, since before he went into care, that he has been the initiator of any kind of romantic gesture. I hold on to the moment. I remember it on days I feel lost to him.

The girls tell me they will be here over Christmas and New Year's. Music, a comfortable wheelchair, an unexpected touch, a kiss, our family together. Such gifts.

The ad for the Westfalia has gone out into the cyberworld. A friend of a friend of a friend, a gentleman from eastern Canada, thinks he might fly out immediately and drive it back to Ontario. I describe our mountain passes in the winter and tell him how many there are between Grand Forks and the Alberta border, never mind the winter winds on the prairies. I suggest he wait until spring has fully arrived. He asks me to research putting it on the train. Just the idea of having to make the complicated arrangements is enough to make me sick to my stomach, and so I apologize and refuse. Our negotiations end.

Ruth, a potter who lives the other side of Nelson, expresses interest. She comes to visit and is obviously keen. She wants to be able to take her grandson camping, and I want that for her, too. The test drive goes well and we settle on the price. It helps to be selling to someone who loves it. We agree that I will store it for her until later in the spring—those darn mountain passes again. Then, while I am backing out of the driveway one morning, the engine bangs and shrieks at me. It has been a little grumpy on the last trips out to charge the battery, but this is a whole new level of protest, one I cannot ignore. At least it's not on fire.

When my mechanic tells me I've seized the engine, that the repair is going to take a while and it's going to be very expensive,

I hardly react. It's just one more thing. It's funny how this works. Two months ago I dreaded selling the van. I was in tears the whole time I cleaned it out. And I dreaded selling the house; part of me still does, but most of the time I just want this all over and done with.

I talk to my older sister, Margaret. She suggests I try reframing my "ifs" as "whens." For example, "If the house sells . . ." becomes "When the house sells . . ."

"If we ever get to Revelstoke . . ." becomes "When we get to Revelstoke . . ."

It is such a simple shift in language but one with huge influence on my thinking. It eases my anxiety and creates happy endings for all the stories I am telling myself.

The van is finally repaired and Ruth still wants to buy it. See? It works!

We meet for the final handover—money exchanged, paperwork complete—on a foul day, windy, wet, and cold. I suspect the Paulson pass is going to be a nightmare and ask Ruth to let me know when she makes it back to Nelson. She emails that evening to say that she is safely home, that the vw runs beautifully, and she loves it very much. I reply with an emoji of a blown kiss.

Ruth immediately responds: *I am so sorry you are sad. You've been through so much. I will treasure it . . .*

I am taken aback until I realize she thinks the little kiss is a teardrop. Now I am horrified to think that she thinks I was "poor-me-ing." Once I've let her know that I really am okay, I laugh about it. And I am okay. Mostly. But I never see a vw Westfalia without a catch of my breath or the wakening of a memory. Sometimes I pat them tenderly as I pass by. I fear that when I am an even older old lady, I will be found beside someone's lovely Westie, forehead pressed to the window, hands planted on either side, peering longingly into the interior and cooing endearments.

"You're beautiful," I'll say. "I love you."

Our girls are anxious for us to make the move to Revelstoke, and I am anxious to get through this period of transition, to feel settled, to breathe out just a little. The dining room table is littered with paperwork and to-do lists, and my head is filled with what-ifs and how-will-I-evers that range from the practical to the irrational.

What if the Revelstoke facility calls with a room for him before I am ready?

What if the house doesn't sell?

How will I ever get us to Revelstoke?

What if I am too old to make new friends?

How will I ever get all our stuff there?

What if he hates it?

What if I hate it?

What if this is a big mistake?

With the house on the market I begin to feel a little of my confidence returning, to think that I've got some of my ducks in a row. I am soon to learn I am dealing with a flock of feckless birds waddling off in all directions.

An offer to purchase comes in quickly, but just as I am wrapping my head around leaving our dear happy place, the deal falls apart. Knowing that I need to get ahead of Lincoln's transfer, I continue with plans to get myself established in Revelstoke. Our friends Jean and Liz offer me temporary housing in a beautiful little cottage on their property on the edge of Grand Forks, above the Kettle River. I can live comfortably there while I pack up the Grand Forks house, shedding belongings and pieces of my heart as I go.

With Parkinson's and stress collecting rocks and storing them in my neck and shoulders, I book a massage and acupuncture treatment because I think it will help. It usually does. However, some poor woman has already arrived at the clinic with a horrible migraine and cannot leave because she is vomiting. When she stops, the doctor comes to see me and manages to get the needles placed before poor migraine woman starts retching again, in the room right next door. She throws up every five minutes for the entire hour I am there. By the time I leave, every muscle in my body has tensed and my stomach is churning in sympathy. Even looking after myself is backfiring.

The packing continues. My sister Margaret comes to help me, walking me through what needs to be done, making lists and meals, and dispensing hugs and encouragement. Kathy and I make trip after trip to the thrift store and Chris takes loads to the dump. Chris and John continue their regular visits to Lincoln, and other friends visit him from time to time. My friend Robbin travels from the coast and packs up all our paintings and other treasures requiring special handling. The girls and their families come home to visit their dad and me and take what furniture, tools, and sports and camping equipment they can use. A nice man from Habitat for Humanity looks at what is left of the tools and building supplies. He returns and completely clears the shed for me, removing all the useless junk as well as the few things they might be able to sell in the Habitat ReStore. It is a huge kindness. Friends show up, unasked, with their shop vac and leave the shed ready for its new owners.

I move into the cottage on Jean and Lizzie's acreage, known among our mutual friends, with great affection, as the Doodle Ranch. My friends own and breed labradoodles, and there are sweet, affectionate dogs, from tiny pups to aging diva-doodles, everywhere.

I finish packing up the house, and with Leora's help, everything I am taking to Revelstoke is transferred to the condo there. Leora does the lioness's share of the work of unpacking and organizing while I loll about, exhausted and overwhelmed. Within the space of two days I have a Revelstoke phone number, a Revelstoke mailing address, a Revelstoke doctor, and a Revelstoke home with my dishes in the cupboards, my towels hanging in the bathroom. *Almost there*, I think to myself.

The one last step is the notice of transfer for Lincoln. On our final day in Revelstoke, Leora and I meet with the young woman responsible for long-term care placements. Her official title is "flow coordinator." We learn that the facility is full and there is a long waiting list.

"Lincoln is safe," she tells us. "We have people waiting for beds who have been many months in acute care in our hospital. We have people still living in the community who are not safe."

She suggests we consider placing Lincoln in Salmon Arm, a larger community with multiple facilities and a shorter waiting time. Salmon Arm is also an hour and a half west of Revelstoke along a particularly nasty stretch of the Trans-Canada Highway.

"It's not an option," I say. "My home is here. He can't go to Salmon Arm without me."

I leave Revelstoke confused and worried but understanding that there might not be a move before the winter. In the meantime, my temporary cottage home is tranquil and cozy and right next door to people I love and who love me.

I return as often as I can to our old house, to muck about in my garden, to kneel among the tulips and irises and all the other growing things I have nurtured year after year. I know there will not be another spring in this garden or underneath the glory that is our ancient crabapple tree in full bloom, but for now, in these moments, I am content. This is work I understand in a small world that makes sense to me, in a place that has not tilted sideways, where sorrow and anxiety are replaced by joy in the discovery of new life poking its way through the soil. The outraged squawking of fledgling crows makes me laugh when I venture too close to the trees they have designated their hangouts. I edge the curves of my flower beds and take satisfaction in the neat frames I am creating around the riot of colour that grows more complex, more vibrant, with each sun-touched day. In the garden, there are no lists, no have-to tasks, there is no grief and no disappointment, no Parkinson's and no dementia, no house inspections to worry about, no bureaucracy to navigate, just sun on my back and the sweet urgency of whim and weather.

My soul needs every bit of the nurturing the garden provides, for when I speak with the staff at Hardy View about the situation in Revelstoke, I can tell they are concerned. I find that unsettling. I wonder what they know that I don't.

Lincoln is pushing the wheelchair during our after-lunch walk one day. He is usually good for a block or two before he freezes and collapses into the wheelchair. However, this time he heads quickly down the first two blocks and across Donaldson Drive, a wide, busy thoroughfare by small-town standards. There is no changing his mind or his direction. His route takes us to the top of Freak Hill, a broad gravel and dirt pathway that connects the subdivision in which Hardy View is located to the fast-food and motel strip in town. He is determined to head down the hill. Freak Hill is, as its name implies, very steep. I have to put my foot down and also play the pity-me-Parkinson's card, because in the unlikely event that we get down the hill without incident, we will never get back up. He reluctantly turns around and walks all but the last block back to Hardy View.

Back in his room, I clip his toenails and trim his beard. I read to him from our old travel diaries. I don't know how much he understands but he seems happy to listen, or snooze-listen. When it is time for me to leave, I try to stand him up so I can transfer him to his bed for a nap. He is not asleep but cannot get his feet under himself. He just walked over a kilometre and now has to be transferred from his wheelchair to his bed by two staff members using a hydraulic lift. Everything about our lives is unpredictable. The only thing I know for sure is that I know nothing for sure.

Several days later, I am told the cleaning staff will be washing the floors in the main part of the cottage, right after lunch. We have to get out of their way. It is raining too hard for a walk, so I wheel Lincoln into his room and am able to transfer him to his bed myself. I put on a Ben Harper CD and lie down beside him. He turns on his side so we can spoon. A staff member pokes her head in the door and sees us both on the bed.

"I'm so sorry!" she says. "I didn't know you were still here. I was just checking on him. I'm sorry!"

"No worries," I tell her. "Nothing more than a cuddle is happening here. Thanks for checking on him." Then I ask her, "What is it the kids do? Hang a sock over the doorknob? So, if you ever see a sock..."

"I always use a necktie," she says, laughing as she closes the door.

While I lose sleep over how or when or if we will get to Revelstoke, my mother spends her evenings on the phone, calling her children one after the other, over and over, her version of robocalling. She has no idea that she has spoken with anyone, and our conversations do little to mitigate her loneliness. We all feel helpless and hopeless as she visits and revisits her sorrow over losing our father. It triggers my own grief over my dad's death and what I will later learn is "anticipatory grief" around losing Lincoln.

Anticipatory grief. The grief I have been experiencing ever since our joint diagnoses in 2011. The grief born of the painful knowing that a life is ending. I know I am already deeply sad, but watching my mother drown in sorrow frightens me. How will I survive Lincoln's death? Will it be as hard for me as it is for my mother?

My brother, Bill, spends many hours each week with her, but she can't remember his visits, even within a single day. I am always in tears when I hang up the phone, riven with guilt for all the things I am not doing for her and for feeling frustrated by her constant interruptions. Even when I don't answer, I know it's her and I know she's unhappy. I am unable to decide which is harder, answering the phone or ignoring it.

I try to compartmentalize my guilt and sadness, to pack it into a mental box and tuck it away for a time when I might have more emotional energy. I tell myself she is safe, in a good living situation, well cared for, and very loved. I tell myself that she and our dad had sixty good years together. My brother and sisters have similar responses, and we all go through times wherein we struggle with a confusion of sadness, frustration, guilt, and helplessness. We are in close communication, especially regarding Mom. It seems that at any one time, there is always someone able to field her calls. We talk about how grateful we are there are four of us. I know I am not doing an equal share of the work, either emotional or practical, that supporting our mom involves. My siblings are understanding. I am glad they are mine.

———

Lincoln has not moved up the list for placement in Revelstoke and is possibly further behind than when we started. In January 2016, I was told to expect to wait six to eight months. Now, in May, six to eight months remains the projection with the caveat of possibly longer. It is no one's fault. There simply aren't enough long-term care beds for the number of people needing them. It is a problem across the province and across the country, one that is only going to get much worse as the baby boomers age.

I make one more trip to Revelstoke, and the flow coordinator repeats the Salmon Arm suggestion. I try to make her understand that I cannot do that; I have to be where he is. Anything else is unthinkable. My home is in Revelstoke and I have made big decisions based on information I was given. She tells me other families have made it work. The important thing is he will be safe.

I'm not other families, I think to myself. *I can't make it work. Is this just about safety? What about quality of life, what about support, what about love?*

I ask her to explain how the list for placement works. She says it is complicated. It is, and I don't really understand.

"Is he ever going to get to come?" I ask.

"Yes," she tells me. "But need has to come first."

How can I argue with that? The conversation leaves me feeling hopeless. We will be spending another winter in Grand Forks, and my cabin is not winterized. I must find a different place to live. Another one of those damn ducks in a row has gone AWOL.

Meanwhile, I accept an offer for the house, but as things progress, I can't find Lincoln's power of attorney document, the one that says I can act on his behalf, the one I need to complete conveyance. There is no simple way to fix this. Lincoln is no longer able to grant power of attorney, and I would have to go through a legal hearing process in order to act on his behalf. That would take months. My carelessness has jeopardized the sale of the house, and so much hinges on that sale. I am sick at heart.

I decide that the missing document must be in my condo in Revelstoke, in a box of files, and ask Sarah to take a look. She is so distressed on my behalf that she can't sleep and gets up in the middle of the night and heads to the condo to search for it. That same night, I wake up suddenly and remember that in the middle of my move to the cabin, I slipped the envelope containing the power of attorney into the tiny space on the floor between the edge of the wardrobe and the wall. You know, for safekeeping.

My relief is very short-lived. I am surprised to hear the voice of Sylvia, the patient care coordinator for Hardy View, on the phone. Her workday should have ended hours earlier; she was supposed to be starting her holidays.

"Leslie, can you take Lincoln home for the night?" she asks me. "We've had some flooding in the building."

"Is he okay?"

"Everyone is okay," she says, "but we need to find places for the residents who've been displaced."

I arrive to find frail, bewildered elders in wheelchairs and sitting on their walkers, crowded together in the few places that offer shade outside the building. It has been a hot day and it is still very warm. They are all strangely quiet, no calling out, no cries of "Nurse, Nurse" or "Help me," none of the usual choruses of confusion and distress. Nurses and care aides are moving among them with purpose. It is a bizarre scene, shocking and upsetting.

I find Lincoln and am met by a nurse. I am asked again if I can take him home.

"Not to my cabin," I say. "I'll never get the wheelchair inside. There isn't room."

"Could you go to a motel? We'll send a care aide to help you."

"I guess so. I'll try."

I call a nearby motel and book a suite with one king-size bed and an alcove containing a second bed. My next call is to Kathy and Chris, who are quickly by our sides. Meanwhile, I learn the bare-bones story of the crisis. A mechanical or electrical failure triggered the sprinklers above the ceilings in three of the five cottages. When the ceilings started to "rain," the charge nurse ordered the whole building evacuated.

Had the evacuation order not been given when it was, or had the staff not acted quickly and efficiently, this could have been an unimaginable tragedy. In the days to come, I am able to get glimpses of the extent of the damage. Great hunks of drywall litter floors and beds and chairs and tables. Huge light fixtures have crashed onto the floor and furniture in common areas, and yet there is not a single injury. I see this for the miracle it is, a miracle worked by a remarkable team of caregivers.

I am handed a bag containing essentials for Lincoln, pyjamas, changes of clothing, adult diapers, a toothbrush, and his medications. I am astonished at the level of organization in the midst of what should be chaos. Kathy and I drive over while Chris pushes Lincoln in his wheelchair to the motel. I am reeling but Lincoln seems calm. It occurs to me that he might be enjoying all this excitement. That would not be out of character. Soon our care aide arrives and Lincoln responds with a smile to her warm greeting, though I have never met her.

"I only work nights," she explains, "so I can be home for my little girl when she's not in school. Lincoln and I are old friends."

I can imagine how well she knows him, my nocturnal wanderer, and I am comforted by her obvious affection for him.

Lincoln and I share the king-size bed through a restless night that I could not have handled on my own. He wakens frequently, sometimes needing to be changed, sometimes just needing reassurance.

"It's me, buddy," I whisper. "We're on a little holiday."

I never thought we would share the same bed again, and I relax to the sound of his breath, his warmth in the bed beside me. In the early morning, while he sleeps, I wrap my arms around him. He feels so familiar and yet so small. The brain scientists tell us that our memories change with every recall, but the feel of him that morning lives in my skin, has sunk into my muscles and bones, unchanged and unchanging, as immutable as stone.

In the morning a member of the recreation team picks us up in the bus and we return to Hardy View. Lincoln's bed has been moved to a hallway in an unaffected area of the building. This is to be his home for who knows how long. He is still able to walk some of the time, is still subject to those episodes of transient loss of consciousness. His present location, beside an outdoor exit and across from the elevator, is not secure. For his safety, a care aide is assigned to him, one to one. I spend more of my days there, freeing Lincoln's care aide to help others.

The projection for the cleanup and reconstruction in the damaged cottages is not weeks but months. From our spot in the hallway, I watch as resident after resident is loaded onto a stretcher and taken by ambulance to other long-term care centres in the Kootenays and elsewhere in the province. I wonder if this might move us up on the list for Lincoln's placement in Revelstoke and am told that there is an ongoing discussion within the health authority about our situation.

One morning, overtired and rushing to get to Lincoln, I mistakenly take a second dose of the handful of pills that start my day. As I am pushing his wheelchair past the nursing station on our way out the door for our walk, my heart begins to race and my head to swim.

Good place to pass out, I think as I slide down a wall.

My little fainting episode may have something to do with it—that and the flood and the crisis it has created at Hardy View and the fact Lincoln lives in a hallway. Perhaps it is the letter I write to Interior Health, or the one to my legislator, or the one to the provincial Health Ministry in which I describe our situation. I don't know the reasons why and I don't have the energy to care. All I know is that on one late-in-July Friday, while I am in Kelowna for a root canal, I get the phone call. Lincoln is now number one on the list for a room at Mount Cartier Court in Revelstoke. Our family is going to be together. It is good news, reason to celebrate, though it distresses me to think that our reunion must come as a consequence of another family's loss.

I know that when we are given an actual date, it will be on very short notice, not more than a couple of days. So many of our friends volunteer to help prepare that I am able to create two teams—one for packing up his room and the other to facilitate transportation to Revelstoke—and two backup teams. I focus on the love and support we are receiving, on the going rather than the leaving. I dare not think about what it means to be tearing ourselves away from Grand Forks with all the connection to place and people that thirty-four rich and happy years have created.

Time enough to grieve when you are settled, I repeat to myself.

I tell Lincoln not that we are moving, but that we are going to Revelstoke to see our girls and our grandchildren. I think he understands. I think he is pleased. I play and replay a movie in my head of how this transition will go, of all the chores and all the goodbyes, all the busy-ness of head and heart to which I must attend.

"Ducks in a row," I whisper hopefully as I check tasks off my many lists.

Kathy and I take Lincoln out for a couple of drives so we can practise getting him in and out of the car. It is hard work, pulling him up out of the wheelchair to stand, pivoting him and coaxing him to bend at the waist so he can settle onto the seat, and then swinging his rigid legs into place. Sometimes he can help us, mostly he can't, and these practice sessions leave both Kath and me dripping sweat in the August heat.

"Good thing I love ya, Linc," she tells him.

It's a good thing she loves us both.

We figure out that it helps to have a blanket on the seat and to tug on it to get him properly positioned for the seat belt. During one practice session, I tug too hard and send him sprawling lengthwise across the entire back seat. As I squeeze into the constricted space to try and set him right side up, I am alarmed to feel him trembling.

"Oh, honey," I say, squirming around to see his face.

It takes me a minute to realize what is happening.

"What the . . . are you laughing?"

And he is.

The day of our move, I show up at Hardy View at 7:00 AM and am greeted by the patient care coordinator, Cynthia, who never got her holidays because of the flood, who is two hours early for work to help me pack up and make sure we have everything we need.

I know there has been pushback in Revelstoke to our transfer, and I do understand why. There are people waiting for the bed Lincoln is going to take, people well known and beloved within that small community, people who have been waiting the better part of a year. Their families are as anxious as I am to have their loved ones settled and safe. I remind myself I've made all my decisions based on what I was told—sold my house, moved everything we own to Revelstoke, prepared for the phone call that seemed less and less likely to come as time went on.

I tell Cynthia I am worried about our reception in Revelstoke.

"There will be good people there, just like here," she tells me. "Just be yourself."

At eight o'clock in the morning on Wednesday, August 12, Kathy and I wheel Lincoln up to the car. As soon as the door is opened, he pops up out of the wheelchair and slides into the back seat, all by himself. He knows exactly what is happening. We are going to Revelstoke. We are going to see our girls. And there is no damn way he is going to be left behind.

I sit beside Lincoln in the back seat while Kathy drives. Our doctor has given us medication that makes him sleepy. As we climb west out of Grand Forks, we are stopped by a herd of cows wandering along the highway at the Eholt summit, taking up both lanes. Cows on the highway. Of course. How very Kettle Valley! Lincoln is calm. Kathy is her usual cheerful, capable self. I don't know what I am. I am not allowing myself to feel anything about this huge transition.

Just get through the day has become my mantra.

The team that packed up the last of his belongings and the few pieces of furniture from his room at Hardy View has worked quickly, and Chris, driving the truck with all our stuff, catches up to us around Rock Creek. Just before Beaverdell, at a sharp bend in the road, we creep past a semi that has tipped on its side, spilling a load of wood chips. At Mara we slow again. This time it is a motorcycle accident. We hear later on the news that the rider walked away unscathed.

When we arrive in Revelstoke, a friendly nurse at Mount Cartier Court, known locally as "the cottages," takes me through the intake process while Lincoln sleeps in his wheelchair beside me.

I soon find that the staff provide what we are used to but don't take for granted: compassionate, skilled, sensitive care. If anyone resents our presence, they hide it well. The setting for the cottages is semi-rural and there are lovely foresty places to walk behind the building. The grandkids visit frequently and are such a hit! The care aides encourage their visits as everyone lights up. Lincoln seems much the same. He has good days, weary days, times when he's aware, and times when he isn't. It is as it has been, moment to moment, day to day.

The day after we arrive in Revelstoke, devastating forest fires rip through our beloved Boundary Country and the South Okanagan. At Kettle River Recreation Area on Highway 33, just north of Rock Creek, the fire moves so quickly that campers are forced to flee on foot, carrying their children, running up the river. Rock Creek and Oliver are devastated by loss. Grand Forks

is on high alert. The highway we travelled just twenty-four hours earlier is closed and remains closed for days to come. We are not the only ones coping with changing circumstances.

8   *The One Who Has to Watch*

WE ARE TWO MONTHS INTO our first year in Revelstoke, and there is a well-established rhythm to our days that makes some kind of sense to me, and, I hope, to Lincoln. I visit twice a day. I help him eat and then we walk.

After lunch on Thanksgiving Monday, I lead us out for a wander in the quiet subdivision near the cottages. I support him with one hand and direct the wheelchair with the other. It is a tricky juggling act. If he freezes, I have just seconds to get the wheelchair under him before he hits the ground. I am getting skilled at recognizing the signs: his steps slow, he stares ahead or down without blinking, he is unresponsive to voice or touch. This state, in the Lewy body dementia literature, is described as a "transient loss of consciousness," but I come across the phrase "transient catatonia," and though it is medically inaccurate, it seems the perfect descriptor for what I see happening to him.

His head is bent forward. It almost always is. He seems as fascinated by light and shadow on the ground, pebbles on the walkway, or his shoelaces as he once was by the horizon or the farthest peak. There is a deer grazing behind the cottages, trees ablaze with gold and crimson, and new snow on the mountains. I feel sad that I cannot find a way to help him lift his eyes to such enchantments. But the day is so beautiful and we are walking together and I natter at myself to not taint the moment with regret. Then he stops, turns his head sideways, and looks at me.

"What's up?" I ask.

"Just checking," he murmurs.

"Checking what?"

"That it's you and me."

It snows in Revelstoke. I've never seen anything like it. It snows and snows and snows. This morning the snow is the perfect packy consistency, so I bundle Lincoln up into warm clothing and wheel him out through the dining room door into the fenced courtyard behind his cottage. He snoozes in the winter sun while I make a snowperson—a lumpy, big-nosed being with pebble teeth defining a goofy grin. It stands in front of the big windows that flank the door, easily seen from inside the cottage.

When we are finished, I enter the code to open the door a number of times, and though the light flashes green, the door won't open. I wave at a few residents who have gathered to watch us. They wave back. I point at the door handle. They smile at me. I wave again. I point again. Wave, point, smile. And on and on.

I am not worried. Lincoln is warmly dressed, and I have my cellphone. There are staff members in the cottage who are just out of sight. But, for a minute or two, I get to enjoy this sweet, funny communication—Lincoln's cottage-mates on one side of the glass and Lincoln and I on the other—and goodwill, affection, and whimsical misunderstanding between us. Wave. Point. Smile.

I don't know many people yet in our new town. A steady, nurturing stream of friends from Grand Forks has wound its way to me, so I should not feel lonely. But I do, not all the time, but a lot of the time. Our girls and their families live here; I see our grandkids almost every day. Sometimes I catch myself in the midst of laying yet another mile of Brio train track or the hundredth reading of *The New Baby Calf*, or remembering which voice to use for the pack-rat puppet, and I catch myself thinking, *We're here. We did it. This is real.* And yet, I am lonely.

An old friend from another life lives here, too. We have made an easy, comfortable connection. She is wise and talented and funny, and I feel beyond lucky to have her living, like our children, just down the street. And yet, I am lonely.

I watch Lincoln's face, and the faces of the other residents in his cottage, when our grandchildren visit, and they visit often. I can't find words for the effect a toddler's laughter has on a group of aging souls lost in dementia. It is transformative. Also transformative—and unexpected—are the moments of quiet, soul-permeating joy of simply being here. And yet, I am lonely.

What is the matter with me?

Logic tells me that in three months you don't make the kind of deep friendships that are forged and burnished over decades. Experience tells me that the measure of my sadness is the measure of the love shared with the truly good people who are, in fact, not so far away. And perhaps it is wisdom that tells me that this joy and this sorrow are not mutually exclusive. I laugh and cry, feel bereft and fulfilled, in the same moment, for the same reason. It's a wonder, this being human.

It is a Sunday morning in late January, and how I wish it were a sun day. Winter has been grey and, lately, very damp. The clouds shroud the mountains, settled and thick, resting on the valley bottom as if they plan to stay forever. I find myself staring out the window, trying to wish them into wisps, peering into the opaque shroud, tormented by the idea of the bright beauty that lies on the other side of this persistent mist.

The streets and sidewalks are bare, however, and that is the silver lining. It feels good to walk easily. I've removed the studded rubber thingies that I pull over the bottom of my boots for better traction. I walk, arms swinging, with long strides and suck in deep breaths of the damp, cold air. I gratefully shed the parkie anxiety that plagues me when I must I pick my way along slippery sidewalks and clamber over heaped-up piles of snow.

Lincoln has been so confined this winter, these past two winters. I don't know how he bears it but he does, with the grace with which he bears all the other indignities of his illness.

We rattle along the side of the road and I hear him speak. I stop and crouch beside him but as soon as the wheelchair stops, he does, too. We repeat this little rattle-mutter-stop-and-go many times over several days. Then I realize what it is he is trying to say. He wants to know who is behind him, who is pushing his wheelchair. When he knows it's me, there is no need for words— and words are almost impossible for him. So now, as we walk, I recite the bits of Shakespeare I remember from high school, my "Parkinshtick" poem, and most of "The Cremation of Sam McGee." I sing old Beatles songs and "Four Strong Winds." We rattle along. He is the silence; I am the noise. It makes me laugh. Some things never change.

I am homesick for Grand Forks. It is a glorious morning after a long winter and a miserable, chilly, rainy, sleety, dust-of-snowy yesterday. In spite of the beauty of the day, or, perhaps, because of it, I walk awhile with sadness, thinking of our old house and backyard. The house was ours but the garden was mine, happily shared but selfishly, obsessively, egotistically *mine*. So much changed in our lives, but the garden, if I did the work, if I loved it hard enough, always flourished. I tended that garden long after I had signed the agreement to sell. I tended it until the day new owners took possession. It was one thing, some days the only thing, that made sense.

There is an ancient crabapple tree in our old backyard. Lincoln used to prune it flattish across the top and spreading wide, a gorgeous parasol of bud, blossom, and leaf, an "Anne with an *e*," White Way of Delight kind of tree. It bloomed only every other year, making it all the more special. I remember the hum of bees, so loud it could be heard in the kitchen if the windows were open. Orgasmically happy bees. And the scent of the blossoms . . . no wonder the bees went crazy.

Sarah and Jason were married under that tree. When Lincoln could no longer prune it, our neighbour Steve picked up the shears and worked his magic. New owners will be enjoying their first spring in our old house, and Barb and Steve have also moved away. It's none of my business, but I wonder if anyone has pruned my tree.

I've longed for spring. I wonder if this self-pity-laden sorrow is what you get when you rue the day and fail to notice the beauty of a dust of snow. Truthfully, I noticed yesterday's dust of snow and had nasty things to say about it. Dear Robert Frost, you were right. I was wrong.

Dust of Snow

The way a crow
Shook down on me
The dust of snow
From a hemlock tree
Has given my heart
A change of mood
And saved some part
Of a day I had rued

Arlo is almost four years old. He visits Grandpa Lincoln every Friday. I help Lincoln with his lunch while Arlo lines up all the tiny, perfect containers of healthy snacks that his mom has packed for him. He opens them carefully, one by one, picks and chooses and nibbles away while charming his granddad and the other dear grandfather who shares Lincoln's table.

Then we take Lincoln out into the sunshine. Arlo pushes the reclined wheelchair until he gets tired. Then he climbs into his grandpa's lap. I curl Lincoln's arms around him and Arlo nestles back against his chest. We stroll and chat. When Arlo falls asleep, this child who never naps, all his big-boy almost four-ness slides back into babyhood, into that innocent, relaxed abandon, one arm flung behind his head, his little legs flopped to the side, warm sun on his face, and loving arms his cradle. Grandpa sleeps, too. They both wear sunglasses—cool shades on my sleeping dudes. We return to the building and make our way through the hallway back to Lincoln's cottage, Grandpa and Arlo still sound asleep. Staff

members, visitors, and a few residents stop to enjoy the moment. I am glad it is not just for me.

It's okay if no one prunes the tree.

By springtime of our first year in Revelstoke, we greet, on our walks, a few regulars who are out with their dogs or pushing strollers. Sometimes we stop to watch as a kayaking guide loads or unloads his dozens of boats. On his aware days, Lincoln smiles at the friendly people we encounter and I am glad to be out in the world with him. As the days grow longer, we add an evening walk to our routines. I think this must be good for him, all this fresh air, but I can never stop mourning, on his behalf, all the joys that are no longer his.

The recreation team at the cottages has a treat in store for us, a bicycle built for two. More accurately, it is a tricycle in reverse. The front two wheels support a detachable wheelchair, and the back wheel responds to pedal power as well as the boost provided by a battery. The brand name is Duet, and I think that is perfect for this remarkable adaptation of a tandem bicycle.

We are the first to use the tricycle, and our maiden pedal takes place on the paved paths behind the cottages. A small crowd of staff members has gathered to watch us. The trike handles beautifully. We fly along the pathways and I take us off-road, across the lawn, because I can, just for fun. The one drawback of the trike is that I cannot see Lincoln's face.

"Are you okay, babe?" I call.

He whoops in answer. There is no mistaking his delight. I am almost delirious with happiness, weeping and laughing at the same time.

There are days when I feel as if I were walking through cement or I cannot still the dyskinesia, uncontrollable dance-like movement caused by my Parkinson's meds. On those days I don't feel confident on the trike, but most days, if it isn't pouring rain, we are out on our new, cool wheels.

In his beautiful and challenging book *Being Mortal*, Dr. Atul Gawande asks his readers to consider models of end-of-life care that are richer, messier, more humane, and more respectful than the institutional models designed for efficiency that prevail in North America. He argues that our current practices, governed by an over-riding principle of risk avoidance, deny personhood, deny joy. He writes, "Our elderly are left with a controlled and supervised institutional existence, a medically designed answer to unfixable problems, a life designed to be safe but empty of anything they care about."[2] I think Dr. Gawande would approve of the Duet tricycle.

I notice that if I take Lincoln out for a trike ride before lunch or dinner, he is able to feed himself or at least partially feed himself. I theorize it is similar to that phenomenon that happens with his speech when he gets upset, but in this situation, his experience on the bike creates endorphins and maybe dopamine. Is it possible being on the trike is giving him a biker's high and the neurotransmitters flooding his brain are making it possible for him to do tasks that are normally impossible? It also makes me wonder to what degree lack of stimulation exacerbates dementia patients' symptoms. I am not a scientist, and Lincoln is just a sample of one, but his time on the bike impacts his life so positively I wish we could give to all dementia patients something as significant to their lives as the Duet is for Lincoln. And yes, it might mean taking some risks. If they could tell us, what would our loved ones lost in dementia want—more years or more joy? Do they have to be mutually exclusive? I know what Lincoln would say.

I hire a young woman to take Lincoln farther afield on the trike once or twice a week. Éliane is strong and smart and very kind. I share with her my sorrow over the lack of excitement in Lincoln's life. She understands him, the things he cared about.

After she has been trained on the trike and taken him out for a few rides, she asks if she can pedal him up to the ski hill and then coast down.

"This is great," she says. "I know I can handle it."

I have always been the cautious one but I never held him back—I couldn't have even if I'd wanted to—and now I have a chance to be bold, for both Lincoln and me. It is hard work to banish the worrisome what-ifs in favour of risk. But I do. And, again, I know what Lincoln would say.

"Go for it!" I tell her.

And she does. She gives him wind in his face and freedom and speed. She gives him back bits and pieces of his old life. They both come home in one piece.

I make many mistakes in the years I am "the boss of us," but this is not one of them. My only regret is that I am not brave enough to go and watch them fly down the mountain.

I have been sick, sick enough to stay in my pyjamas, sick enough to stumble as far as the couch and no farther, and far too sick to go anywhere near Lincoln or my grandchildren for almost a week. A night spent sleeping soundly and breathing more easily in my own bed, instead of shifting position in the recliner, marks a corner turned, the virus in slow retreat.

I wake to an apartment really in need of a haz-mat team and with enough energy to pretend to be one . . . in fits and starts. Between naps, I strip the bed, including the mattress and duvet covers. I don't remove the duvet cover easily—not that removing it is hard. It is the putting it back on that daunts me, but this one has been wet-sneezed on, coughed into, and used to wipe sweat from breaking fevers. It has to come off. It has to be washed. And dried. And put back on.

As I struggle to turn it inside out and find the bottom corners, blindly following the feel of the side seams while drowning in metres of patterned percale, I am hit with a memory.

The same duvet cover but a different bed, a different home, a different life . . .

The duvet and cover have been out on the clothesline during a spring cleaning blitz. I spend a few minutes blissfully inhaling that gorgeous, outdoor-clean-linen scent before calling Lincoln to help me make up the bed. In our house, it is always a two-person job and we have it down to a science, an easy step-by-step process we have perfected over our years of changing bedding together. But this time is different; Lincoln is lost, anxious to help but unable to figure what to do or to follow my instructions.

"It's okay, honey," I tell him. "I think I've got this."

I manage to get the cover inside out and smooth on the bed. I climb onto the bed and, on my hands and knees, stick my head into the open bottom edge, walk my hands down the side seams, and find the top corners. I hop off the bed while clinging to the corners and pick the bottom edge of the duvet up off the floor by its corners. This is when I remember I am unable to raise my arms above my head; one shoulder is in recovery from a rotator cuff repair, and the other is waiting for the same surgery. There is no way I am going to be able to hold the duvet up while I try to slip the inside-out cover over it, flipping it right side out as part of the process. I am explaining this so badly. That seems appropriate to the situation.

Lincoln hovers, chuckles, lifts bits of fabric, and gives gentle, not always helpful tugs. I finally hop up onto the bed and from shoulder height let the whole mess fall from my fists to the floor while trying to shake the cover over the duvet. At this point I should factor in Parkinson's balance challenges and positional tremor. When I extend my left arm, the whole darn thing shakes. I hop off the bed onto the floor in order to finish the job, and as I wipe sweat from my brow and button the last button, Lincoln says,

"Thank goodness. I'm glad that's over!"

"What? *You're* glad?" I say and start to laugh.

"I had to watch!" he says.

That cracks me up. And Lincoln, too. I howl with laughter. My laughter is loud. Loud, raucous, snorty, and unladylike. Lincoln doesn't laugh out loud. Even his biggest laughter is almost silent—a hilarious combination of snuffles and uh-uh-uhs from deep in his throat that our girls delight in imitating—but his face crinkles into something magical and gleeful and remarkably contagious.

But, as I laugh, sorrow catches me off guard. It takes me a moment to realize this is more than just an acknowledgement of how deeply the veins of silliness run through our life together. It tells another truth. He is right. It is hard to be the one who has to watch.

My sister Jane and my nephew take two ferries and drive the Malahat highway to get from the Sunshine Coast to Victoria. They come to hug our mom, who is in the hospital recovering oh so slowly, as only a weary ninety-five-year-old can, from a hip broken in two places. They have also come to pick up my niece, who lives and works in Victoria, so that their family can all be together for the high school graduations of "the littles," my twin nephew and niece. I meet them at the hospital for a brief, lovely visit.

Hello.

Goodbye.

I love you.

They miss their final ferry home by just minutes, and it is late, late, late when their travel day finally ends. After Jane leaves, Mom asks about her many times. I tell her that Jane and the big kids were here, that they came all that way, that our older sister, Margaret, was here all last week and will be returning soon, that my brother, Bill, is with her every single day.

"Oh, I am such a bother," she says again and again. "Tell Lincoln thank you for letting you come."

Oh, Momma.

Then she wants to know where my siblings are, and I tell her all over again.

She has to wait a long time to be taken to the bathroom. I understand the pressure the staff are under, but it upsets me to see her in such distress. When my big brother arrives I vent to him. When her nurse shows up, my brother calls her "an overworked angel." She is so disbelieving that she asks him to repeat it, her face softening toward tears as she realizes he is sincere. He then thanks a male nurse, who tells him how rare such expressions of gratitude are. That same nurse later asks me who the "tall guy" is. He tells me how much he appreciates being acknowledged.

My mom's friend Liz comes to visit her. They have been pals since 1953. Liz comes on her own, pushing her walker and bearing gifts. She is, as my brother describes, "lively, irreverent, and fun." She lights up the room and my mom, my brother, and me. She leaves some of that light behind.

My brother squats down in the moving elevator to talk to an old soul in a wheelchair.

"How are you?" he asks her.

"Still standing," she whispers.

"You look beautiful," he tells her.

Her smile is . . . I don't have words for her smile.

I call Margaret, who is back in Vancouver, to fill her in on Mom's progress. Margaret is our agreed-on contact with the intermediate care facility that is my mom's home. She is the one who figures out the next steps, even though we can only do this one step at a time. She has the people who need to talk to each other talking to each other.

Tomorrow morning our friend John will rise early and drive from Grand Forks to Tsawwassen. He will pick me up at the ferry dock, then turn around and drive me to Revelstoke. Then he will drive himself back home. That's about nineteen hours of driving.

Today, at the end of my last day with my mom, my brother takes me up to the top of Mount Tolmie. I look out over the city all the way to the ocean and the Olympic Peninsula.

"I thought you might like a look at the big picture," he says.

As our days in Revelstoke become months and almost a year, I find myself grateful our bewildered family is together but am sometimes sad with the missing of home. My daily visits to the cottages are my anchor in a strange, disconnected life. I help Lincoln eat and take him for walks. I read to him and show him photographs and tell him our stories, but I do not know what he knows. I know that he is always happy to see me, our girls, and our grandchildren, because his face lights up with a smile so bright and so fleeting that I am both suffused with delight and almost undone. Sometimes he sighs in greeting, and then he is gone. His eyes close; his head droops; his thoughts and feelings slip far beyond guessing.

When I return after visiting my mother, I wrap him in a hug.

"I missed you every day," he murmurs, the longest sentence he has said in a great while.

The disease has almost silenced him, but sometimes I get this precious whispering of meaningful words. I write them down on scraps of paper. I still find them on occasion, ragged fragments out of time.

As I hug him, he slides his arm around my waist and pats my back, a rare, remembered touch that carries the comfort of all our together years. I feel that touch still, in the small of my back. When he grows tired, I settle him into his wheelchair and he disappears from me once more.

"Goodbye, buddy. I love you," I whisper at the end of that visit, at the end of every visit.

I buy a loveseat for his room so I can sit beside him instead of crouching by his wheelchair. He leans into me and then closes his eyes. Asleep? I never know for sure. I wear his familiar weight and listen to our old CDs. The music conjures memories. I wonder if it does for him.

I pull him to his feet after helping him with meals. I want him to walk a bit, to get out of the wheelchair. We wait for the message from brain to limbs to. make the journey through the bizarre neuron jams.

"Okay, feet! Start walking!" I say.

I rub his legs and tap his toes with my fingers. I rock him gently back and forth. And then, sometimes, he doesn't just find the familiar shuffle—he hops. He hops from one foot to another! He bounces! He skips! He laughs out loud!

As he boogies, I hold on for his dear life because he falls frequently. He . . . we . . . make the staff anxious. They've all seen me go sideways when I mean to go forward. I beg for his freedom to move, for our right to move together, and they let it be. For the time being, they let it be.

We start dancing together in his room. The first time that I hold on to his hands and coax him to stand so we can dance, he joins me not with that exuberant hopping-bopping-bursting-out of his own volition but with a sweet little shuffle. We dance in that small space. We dance to "Yellow Submarine," "Bennie and the Jets," and "Diamonds and Rust"—three songs, and the last one a slow one—and I am, for a moment, back in our old, good life, in his arms, home again.

In the fall of 2016, a year after we move to Revelstoke, I attend the World Parkinson Congress in Portland, Oregon. Even though I travel with Leora, who puts her life on hold to accompany me, it is a very complicated time. *In the Red Canoe* is released the same week, and I am away from Lincoln for the longest period of time since he went into care. Early in the morning, the first day of the congress, CBC Radio announces that I have won its creative non-fiction prize for a personal essay, "Adaptation," the story of that scary night with Lincoln at the movies and the walk along the river.

I miss the opening sessions of the congress because of publicity responsibilities to the CBC, and by the time I make it to the conference centre that afternoon, I am feeling distinctly parkie—exhausted, shaky, off balance, flat—and questioning the kind of person I am for not feeling the joy I ought to be experiencing, when everyone I know and love is so happy on my behalf.

I walk into the main exhibition hall of the conference centre and the first things I notice are the displays by the pharmaceutical companies. I know that the medications I take make it possible for me to walk, to dance, to ride my bike, to feed Lincoln, to hold my grandbabies in my arms, to type my stories, and even to be in Portland. I am deeply grateful. But as I look at all the shiny displays and the shiny salespeople distributing literature and goody bags, I feel my head explode a little bit.

We are very big business!

And on that cynical note, I turn and walk out of the building. I sit in the plaza in the sunshine and try to settle myself down, to talk myself into a more positive frame of mind. I people-watch, picking out who I think might be the doctors, the scientists, the advocates, the salespeople, the family members, and of course the other parkies. My heart breaks for some, and I sink emotionally lower with each passing moment. Then a tiny little woman stops nearby. She stands there and does not move. I guess that she is "off," frozen in place, and struggling to get her brain to tell her legs to move again. I walk over to her and ask if she needs help.

"I've lost my . . ." She searches for a word. "My sticks," she says in English with a strong Hispanic accent.

"Your sticks?" I ask. "Your crutches?"

She nods.

"How can I help?"

"Do you speak Spanish?"

I offer her my arm and we stand there. After a few minutes she manages to push a foot forward and then the other, and we shuffle together into the building. I find her a bench on which to rest and go off in search of help. I am soon leading a conference volunteer, a young woman who speaks Spanish and English, back to my little lady. Within minutes the volunteer has organized the delivery of new crutches and searched out our little lady's friends.

"I'll stay with her until everything is sorted out," she tells me.

I hug them both, blubber a little bit, and head back outside to the plaza. I need to collect myself, one more time.

Something shifts inside of me because of my brief connection to that brave, small person. She is the unwitting agent of a profound change. Despite all her challenges, and without the very tools that propped her up, she still tried to meet her goals for the day. She trusted in kindness and let me help her a little. In return, she helped me so much more.

I don't like having Parkinson's. It often makes me self-conscious and uncomfortable in public places, but I need to keep going out. The alternative is no way to live. I sit in the plaza with the warm sun on my face and count my blessings. That helps. I think of the tiny little woman, and that helps. I people-watch, and that helps most of all. I see past staring eyes and frozen faces, right into the heart of courage. My former sadness becomes admiration and awe.

Thank you, I silently call, to every parkie who passes by.

––––––––––––––

Sorrow is a constant in my story, as it is in so many people's stories. And I worry. What if this sorrow is the intimation of a darkness with which I will have to contend one day? I know the statistics on Parkinson's and depression. Sometimes I feel cornered by just the thought of those black dogs.

One day I go, as I do every day, to visit Lincoln. One of the care aides pulls me aside as I enter his cottage.

"Oh, Leslie," she says, her eyes crinkling with mirth, "I have to tell you a story."

She says that Lincoln woke late, and when she last checked, he was still in bed. She sat at a small workstation near his room, working on reports and listening for him. Her partner went into Lincoln's room, came out immediately, and asked where he was.

"He's in bed!" she said.

"No, he's not," her co-worker replied.

They both went into his room, puzzled and a little anxious. And then they heard him. He was behind the door, fully aware that they were looking for him, and he was laughing.

"I've never heard him laugh like that!" she says, laughing herself as she tells me. "We had to hold him up he was laughing so hard. The three of us were laughing so hard. It was so great. It was amazing. I almost peed my pants."

I think this is what happened that morning. He crawled out of bed and found himself in the corner, behind the door. He often finds himself, and I often find him, standing in corners. To his delight, his caregivers showed up and he got to give them that little moment of anxiety. This is a wonderfully perfect, Lincolnesque moment. And a reminder to me that something essentially himself, joyful, spirited, and fun-loving, still lives inside him.

Lewy body dementia and Parkinson's disease have much in common, and our stories may resolve in ironically similar ways, Lincoln's and mine, but at this time, his takes him into actual corners and mine into metaphorical ones. The difference is that he laughs from his.

Theron and Naomi are leaving the dining room in Lincoln's cottage. He waves at his grandpa and me from his perch in her arms, and I wave back. A staff member calls her goodbyes. Theron beams and waves with delight, and soon everyone in the cottage has joined in. He is a tiny rock star, a little prince, a bringer of light.

Essey Celeste is Sarah and Jason's little one, Arlo's baby sister. She is named after Lincoln's lovely mom—though Sarah has decided to spell her name differently—and Queen Celeste from the Babar books. I was able to leave Lincoln for three days with Marilyn, our

kind night nurse, in order to be present for her birth and spend time with Arlo. Essey is almost a year old by the time we move to Revelstoke. She and her mom visit Lincoln three mornings a week, after they drop her big brother off at preschool. I show up at the cottage and find her sitting beside Grandpa Lincoln on a sofa in the lounge and clutching her monkey finger puppet. She is so small there is room at her feet for the stack of board books we keep in Lincoln's room for the kids to read when they visit. He is sitting more erect than usual and one hand gently rests on her wee foot. A hint of a smile can just barely be seen as he angles his head in her direction. There is such comfort between them. When it is time for her to leave her grandfather, who is now in his wheelchair and fully reclined, Essey carefully tucks a flannelette square under his chin to catch the drool. She seems impossibly small for such gentle caregiving.

Sarah and Arlo join Lincoln and me for Christmas dinner in Lincoln's cottage. The dining room, in fact the whole building, is wonderfully decorated. The kitchen staff have outdone themselves and serve up turkey and gravy and mashed potatoes and green beans and stuffing and salads and cranberries and pie. Lincoln has been dressed up for the occasion and sports a Christmas tie. Arlo is wearing a sweater that Lincoln's mom knit for Sarah's first Christmas. It is bright red with a sequined Christmas tree smack in the middle of the front. Essie knit Sarah's name in large white letters into the bottom ribbing. It's too small for Arlo but he loves it, and wisely his mother lets him wear it. Lincoln is alert and happy, able to feed himself with just a little help. There is a visit from Santa and treats for a little boy.

On Christmas morning the girls, Theron, Arlo, and I visit Grandpa. Our wee boys go from resident to resident, passing out cards and craft foam gingerbread men decorations they helped their mothers make. The biggest gifts are the smiles connecting old to young.

Joy to the world.

It's a cold January day but bright and sunny, rare enough during the Revelstoke winter, which seems to be snow, snow, and more snow. I borrow cross-country skis from Sarah and dress warmly before heading out to the golf course trail with new friends. As I put on my gaiters I notice that one of them now bears a hand-written label. That must have happened sometime during the last winter in which Lincoln lived at home.

That was the winter we switched from skis to snowshoes. That was the winter we spent a month in Revelstoke, over Christmas and New Year's, trying out the new condo. That was the winter I drove the Paulson pass behind the snowplow while Lincoln fussed with the CD player and couldn't make it work, and I couldn't help him; I didn't dare take my eyes off the road or my hands off the wheel. That was the winter of the "imposter" Leslie, the malevolent stranger who, in Lincoln's eyes, looked like me but was not me. That was the winter of frantic visits to the doctor, to the emergency room, of rethinking all our plans, of learning how to ask for help. And that was the winter of friends rallying around, spending the night, taking him out, checking in on both of us, holding us close, and holding me together. That was the winter he must have labelled the gaiter. "LEFT," it says in shaky, childlike printing done in black felt pen.

Tomorrow, like today and every day, I will visit my husband. I wish I could share with him the story of the gaiter. I wish I could gently tease him and we could laugh together. Instead, I will hug him and tell him that we raised wonderful girls. I will tell him that we sometimes made each other crazy but we were never bored. I will tell him that he is the love of my life. And though it doesn't matter, not one bit, which leg wears that labelled gaiter, I will always wear it on the left.

I am reading *Fallen: A Trauma, a Marriage, and the Transformative Power of Music* by the writer Kara Stanley. Kara tells how her husband, Simon, wrote with his weak left hand as part of his recovery following a traumatic brain injury. For two weeks I have been close to finishing *Fallen* but find I can handle only a few pages at a time. This slow reading is no fault of Kara's. It is a beautiful book, honest and brave, and it unravels me, again and again. It would have before Parkinson's disease, before Lewy body dementia, but not like this. So much of Kara's story strikes chords of loss, of fear and exhaustion, of family and friends who rise above and rise above again, and of the search for what is home when the centre shifts.

So I am writing with my left hand, my parkie hand. I tell myself that this is good for my brain. I will write one page today and another tomorrow and the next day and the next. I am writing these words, right now, with my left hand. It is hard to hold on to my thoughts at this slow speed. Being forced to slow down is also, probably, good for my brain.

Outside the snow falls in straight lines, like white rain. I am glad for the snow. Revelstoke is beautiful in the snow. Enough has fallen that I will try out, for the first time, the little skis that clamp on to the front wheels of Lincoln's wheelchair and will hopefully allow us to get outside. It was hard work to find those skis. I spent many hours on the computer and on the phone tracking down a supplier. I hope they are worth it, because half a centimetre of snow is enough to stop us in our tracks and I cannot bear the thought of him spending another winter confined to the cottage, without respite in the fresh air, without wind on his face or the chance to catch a glimpse of Mount Cartier, a startling arrowhead of white against the blue, blue sky.

I sit here beside the tiny potted fir that is my Christmas tree. The gas fireplace chases the morning chill from the living room. I sit here in all this comfort and I am feeling rueful about a wasted

yesterday. I had returned with some excitement to a manuscript for a picture book on which I have been working for ages. I left it so much worse than I found it and did not walk or lift weights or practise yoga or cook anything healthy for the coming, busy week. I went to bed frustrated and feeling guilty about neglecting the work I do to manage my Parkinson's—and annoyed about the necessity of paying constant attention to my parkie self and how I am doing.

This morning I read a few more pages of *Fallen* and am humbled, as I always am, by Kara and Simon's grace and strength.

It makes me want to write again about Lincoln's grace and strength and how it is revealed in his laughter. I want to tell, one more time, how he has always been a quiet, almost silent chuckler—perhaps, as with so many things about our relationship, to provide balance for my loud, cackling outbursts. I want to tell that he has always been an easy smiler, and oh my goodness, the sweetness of his smile. It softens his craggy, lean features and brings such warmth to his brown eyes. Despite his disease, he still smiles frequently. It stops his caregivers in their tracks.

"That smile, Leslie!" they say.

I know exactly what they mean. I am reminded what hard jobs they do and how little time they have to just be present with the fragile souls for whom they care. They must feel very empty sometimes. I am glad for Lincoln's smile in their lives, too.

But Lincoln's laughter is something more. It has always been a rare occurrence, and like all rare and lovely things, it is to be treasured. These days he laughs most in the presence of our grandchildren. At ages four, three, and two, they have no memory of him except as a resident in a long-term care home. They move through his space with the ease of familiarity. They adjust his footrest, push his chair, tuck the cloth beneath his chin to catch the drool. They show him their drawings, their Lego buildings, and their stuffies. They tell him their stories. He knows they are ours. They can be happily loud, and that is when he laughs the hardest. His delight in their presence, his laughter, fills my leaking emotional bucket with a blessedness I do not take for granted.

Lincoln now must contend with huge physical startles. The clinical term is "myoclonic jerks." I read that they present in late-stage Lewy body dementia. Late stage. The words unglue me. I know well where he was three years ago and I know well where he is today. Late stage is a reality I thought I had accepted, and then I realize I have no idea what acceptance means. Whatever it is, it does not deny the grief.

When a seizure grips him, Lincoln's arms and legs shoot out and his whole body lurches forward with such force that, were he not seat-belted in, he would be flung from his chair. I lean over him, hug him, and reposition his arms and legs, more to comfort myself than to help him. I fight tears and inwardly rage that he must contend with this as well. But he laughs. He laughs as if this betrayal of brain and body were just another enormous joke—this day's version of tumbling over the handlebars of his bike or bungee jumping naked from a bridge. His laughter lights up my dark places.

And as for the little skis for his wheelchair, it is hard work to figure how best to get them attached to the front wheels and make them stay on. I have help from the recreation team, and we think we have figured it out. The first time I try them by myself, one of the skis falls off just feet from the door. I phone Andrew, the recreation coordinator, and he is able to reattach it. The next time it happens, I am several blocks away. I kneel beside the wheelchair and struggle to hold the ski still with one hand while I try to tug the wheelchair forward with the other. It soon becomes clear that isn't going to work. I then brace the ski with my knee and am able to use both hands to position the chair and the wheel on the ski. The next step is to clamp the ski in place, but between the cold and my tremor, I can't close the clamp.

A big black truck pulls up beside me—Alberta plates, snowmobile in back. I must confess I often have indulged in unkind thoughts about big trucks with Alberta plates and their "sleds." A young woman hops out of the truck.

"Do you need some help?" she asks.

I show her what I am trying to do. She easily closes the clamp.

"These are very cool," she says, examining the skis. "I think I see why this one came off. It's not set at the same width as the other."

"Oh, dear! That has to be adjusted with a screwdriver," I explain. "I didn't bring one."

She hops up and goes to her truck, returning a few minutes later with a screwdriver with multiple bits. She finds the right size and adjusts the setting. After thanking her, I push the wheelchair back toward the cottages. She drives slowly beside me, not leaving us until I turn into the driveway. Now when I see a big truck with Alberta plates and a sled in back, I think of her and her kindness.

With the ski problems resolved, we are able to get outside often that winter. That lights up my dark places, too.

When I was little, I sometimes heard a shushing in my ears, just as I was falling asleep. I imagined it was an angel whispering my name. It meant I was not alone, that something wondrous and beautiful watched over me in the dark. I think of that from time to time and wish I could still hear those angel voices.

Lincoln can no longer speak. That has been our reality for a long time now. Every once in a while, there is a word or phrase that is clear and meaningful, but as the disease progresses, these have become fewer, the time in between measured in weeks and months. But in the last couple of days, while I have been coaxing him to open his mouth for soup or pudding or green-blob-this or white-blob-that, he has merrily called out, "Hello!" or "Come in," clear as a bell. In his old voice.

I am good at entering his world. Or, I am good at pretending to enter his world. I need to be. For all the love I bear, I cannot carry him into mine. So I acknowledge his greetings. He calls, "Hello!" and "Hello!" I say.

"Come in," he says.

"Thank you. It's lovely to see you."

It is so easy at the time, and it is only after, when I get home, weary and alone, that I feel the desolation that I cannot know who it is he sees or hears, that it has been so very long since we truly inhabited the same world.

Our friends John and Mary Ann are visiting this week. As John leans in to tell Lincoln stories of their shared adventures and misadventures, to kindly tease him with memories of their Lost Boy days, Lincoln opens his eyes and leans in to listen. His eyes focus, his mouth finds the rare and precious smile, and a connection is made, for long and extraordinary minutes, a connection that is undeniable in its power and truth. Mary Ann bears witness, too, as do the care aides. We all need the tissues from the box that is passed around. In his cottage, staff members who witnessed it are still telling their colleagues about it and getting teary-eyed all over again.

Angels still whisper in my ear.

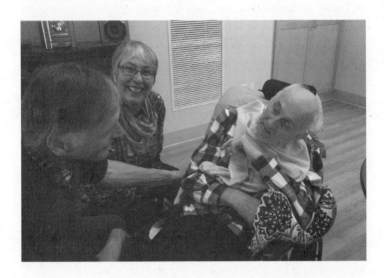

She was born on a snowy night in late December, Naomi and Isaac's baby girl, Theron's little sister, beautiful and perfect, the best gift of the season. Maisie Jane.

When she was just weeks old, she got sick with a scary respiratory virus and spent a week in the neonatal intensive care unit in the Kamloops general hospital, three hours away from home. It was an awful time, but our tiny girl recovered and came home to us.

Lincoln sleeps a lot these days, and when Naomi and Maisie visit him, he doesn't always respond. When he does, his face softens. His smile blooms.

In a photo taken soon after their return from the hospital, Naomi is holding Maisie up so Lincoln can see her. Taken from the side, it shows the delight on her grandpa's face as he drinks her in, as her blue eyes meet his in curiosity. There are many photographs of Theron, Arlo, and Essey with Lincoln, and few of Maisie. Their lives will overlap for only six short months. I am grateful he got to meet her. I am grateful to have the photo.

"That's you," I'll tell her later. "This is my favourite picture of you and Grandpa Lincoln. Can you see how much he loves you?"

"Yes," she nods. "Can we play now?"

Somewhere Lincoln is beaming.

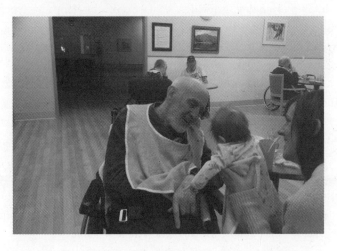

We are well into our second year in Revelstoke, Lincoln's third year in care. I want to bring him home to live with me. Not because his caregivers in the cottages aren't skilled and kind—they are. There aren't enough of them, but that is the nature of health care, isn't it, in this rich, beautiful country. There is enough of me, though, and so I am with him every day, most days twice a day, and our girls and our grandchildren are there as often as they can be, and that translates to many visits a week. But I still want to bring him home.

When Lincoln first went into Hardy View it was because I couldn't keep him safe or myself in good health. His interior world was changing so rapidly, his exterior one shifting and warping in ways I could not understand. I had frightening, unsettling glimpses of what he was experiencing from time to time, but no one knows, no one can know, what it must be like to find oneself lost in familiar places, confused by those you have always loved. And because he had always been so fit and strong and independent, he clung to his physical abilities far longer than most do with his disease. Restless nights and restless days . . . hours spent planning, thinking, arranging, grieving . . . alarms on the door . . . hypervigilance . . . and exhaustion. I did what I had to do and thought I would die of guilt and sorrow. We both settled into our new realities and I found a way to some measure of acceptance.

He can no longer walk, so the bitter irony is that he is safe. Safe and silent. So why not bring him home?

I have this picture in my head of him here in the little condo we bought together and in which he never got to live. I have this picture of him snoozing in his wheelchair while I cook or clean or read or write, and whenever he opens his eyes, there I am, or there someone else who cares about him will be, and he will never be alone in his room and I will never wonder again if he is all right. Our family and friends will visit and he will be home. Home with me.

It seems not simple but doable, and there are programs that

support the desire. The work involved is daunting, but I tell myself I am up to it. I hold on to that picture in my head. A team of health-care professionals quickly organizes to help me explore the possibility. If the team members think I am crazy, they never make me feel that way. They meet with me and meet with me again. They give practical advice. They research and ask questions and find the answers. I read Health Ministry websites by the hour; I talk to family and friends and people who have made similar situations work. I wake up in the middle of the night and crunch numbers, trying to find the money necessary to pay for enough help, for long enough, because if I do this, it cannot fail. There will not be a place for him in care. We will be back in waiting-list purgatory. I know that.

I hold on to that picture in my head. And then I have to let it go. In the end, it is too big for me, for too many reasons. I am not a business person and it would be just that, a small business, with a number of employees, sharing our space twenty-four hours a day, all deserving of decent pay for work that demands such a high level of trust and empathy and patience.

Love does not conquer all. It does not double my income or turn me into someone who is a competent manager of others. It does not turn back time so Lincoln can complete a representation agreement, a necessary step along the way. It does not increase the size of our living space or find the perfect helpers in a community that is, like so many, under-resourced when it comes to health-care workers.

It's not that it's impossible. I know a different me could make it work. I know that. Someone smarter, perhaps, or more disciplined, someone stronger or more persistent could make it work. This is the hard part, acknowledging my limitations, and it isn't just about having Parkinson's. It is about feeling that I have failed him again.

When I started the process, I told myself and others I knew it was a long shot, that I was simply exploring the possibility. I was telling what I thought was the truth. Truth is, I made that picture in my head and it hurts to let it go. It diminishes me.

I must make another picture. Our girls will help with that. Our grandkids, too. Family and friends inspire gratitude for their continued, loving commitment to walking this path with us. I start to tilt sideways and they hold me up. That helps. Another picture will have to find its way through this sadness. I just don't know what it will be.

It is late, after 8:00 PM, and I am hungry because I have not yet eaten. After Lincoln's dinner I took him for a walk. There are no mosquitoes yet. The last rays of sun gilding the snow on top of Mount Cartier and the perfect temperature kept us out extra long. When I stop for groceries on my way home, two bags of Orville Redenbacher's sweet and salty popcorn jump in my cart and will not leave. Hungry shopping is always a bad idea!

A young man with a basket containing a few items stands behind me in the lineup at the till, and I ask him to go ahead. He does not meet my eyes for longer than a second but quietly says, "Are you sure?" and then "Thank you."

I notice the crumbling foam sleeping mat attached to his faded canvas pack. He pulls coins out of his pocket and counts them twice. Everything about him seems to speak to struggle and poverty. I slip around to the other side of the till and ask the cashier to include his bill with mine. This is not generosity—it makes no difference to me, costs me money I can easily spare.

The news this morning, June 3, 2017, repeatedly told how Chrissy Archibald, a young woman from Castlegar, was killed in a terrorist attack on a bridge in London, England. I have been thinking about her all day and her family's kindness campaign, their response to this tragic loss. How do people devastated by that kind of grief rise so high? I am grateful to have an opportunity to respond standing right in front of me.

When the cashier refuses his payment, and explains why, he seems bewildered and then turns to me.

"It's okay," I say. "I needed to pay something forward."

"Thanks," he says and disappears out the door.

It makes the cashier cry.

"I have a son . . ." she says.

"I didn't mean to make you cry," I say, and I tell her about Chrissy and her family.

When I get home, I realize that my cellphone is still in the bag on the back of Lincoln's wheelchair and set to ring for my final pill of the day at 10:00 PM. Waiting until the morning to go in is not an option.

The cottage is quiet and the lights dim when I return. Lincoln is in bed, comfortably positioned. He opens his eyes when I tiptoe in. I pick up my phone and the also-forgotten bag of rhubarb, a gift from Joan, whose husband shares Lincoln's table. When I bend over to whisper good night and I love you, he closes his eyes and he smiles. My turn for tears.

I lie in bed and think of all of us, Lincoln and me, the young man, the cashier, beautiful Chrissy, and all who mourn her, and how our connections spiral out into the world in infinite webs of joy and sorrow and suffering and grace, and how it is all too big to comprehend and yet each piece is so small.

Lincoln has lost the ability to dance. I can coax him into standing, but he looks at his feet with bewilderment. Soon he is unable to bear his own weight. He begins sleeping most of the time and grows increasingly rigid, almost impossible to dress or change. The staff wrap him in warmed flannel sheets as he curls into himself.

Then he stops eating. He takes water in tiny sips or slivers of ice. His eyes seldom open.

I move into his room and sleep on a cot, face to face with him. He wakes in the night. How frightened he seems, wide-eyed and staring into a distance I cannot measure at something I cannot see. I lean over him and stroke his face.

"I am here, my love," I whisper. "I am always going to be here."

I grieve for all the times he must have been awake in the night, frightened, and I was not there.

After they change his position, his caregivers haul the heavy furniture around, more than once, more than twice, so I can face him still and rest my hand on his chest and feel the beat of his amazing, persistent heart. I listen to his laboured breathing and startle fully awake with every break in the rhythm. I tell him our stories.

"Hey, babe," I whisper into the dark. "I was thinking about Morocco . . . that time in the mountains . . . the Berber women and Henna Baby, Monsieur le Maire . . . I wonder how their lives turned out . . . I wonder . . . "

I stop speaking if I start to cry.

I tell him the girls are coming, they will be here soon, and he breathes a loud, contented sigh. Our daughters join us every day and, sometimes, the grandkids. We camp in his room and friends bring meals and kindness. How strange it is to think that these beautiful women, my new tribe, will never know him, how everyone I have met in the last few years, and everyone I will ever meet, will never know him.

His daughters and I, we take turns lying beside him. We weep and comfort one another. We talk to him and we talk about him and we often laugh. Kathy and Chris, our friends-who-are-family, travel from Grand Forks to share in the waiting. We play his favourite music and dance our baby Maisie around the room.

When one of the nurses suggests that perhaps my constant

presence holds him here, I tell her that he's always done things his own way.

"If he's here, he wants to be. I'm not leaving."

This is about me, too, I think, and then I am ashamed of my selfishness.

"We'll be okay," I tell him. "I'll be okay."

It's the best I can do.

How strangely beautiful he grows, and I cannot help but think of his "angel self." His skin becomes smooth, his brow unwrinkles, his constricted limbs slowly unfold and relax, as the medicine that takes him far away from us and into deep, deep sleep gives ease to his pain and gentles the journey for my weary, brave traveller.

He dies on a summer Sunday, just before sunset, during that exquisite hour of long shadows. He dies when our girls go briefly home to tend to their families and our friends are out for dinner. He dies when we are alone.

He dies and I hear my voice as if it belonged to someone else.

"Oh buddy. Oh buddy."

Over and over.

Oh buddy.

9   *And What of Grace?*

I WANT TO REMEMBER that the music I chose, by chance, to play when I did not know we had just minutes left was a CD made for us years ago by Naomi. *Travelling Tunes*, she named it, and she drew a picture of a VW Westie for the cover. After he left us, we listened, my girls and I, we three who loved him and had just lost him, we listened to "Rise Again" by the Rankin Family. He loved that song. Whenever it played, he said, "I want that at my funeral." Only he doesn't want a funeral, he wants something simple and happy, a party. That is what we will try to give him. A party.

I want to remember waking that first morning after he died and standing on my balcony, looking at the sun on Mount Begbie.

"Are you there?" I ask him.

And the answer comes back. "I've gone to Grand Forks but I won't be long."

"Your 'won't be long' or my 'won't be long'?"

I want to remember the morning walk when two eagles soar above the river. I have been weeping over photos and find one I do not remember but that delights me—two exuberant, aging Lost Boys, one with a cloud of white hair about his head and the other wearing a white hat. They stand, their arms flung out against the sky, atop enormous pinnacles of rock. David and Lincoln on Gimli. Photographed by John. And then the eagles, just hours later. Flying free. Together. I prefer my thinking magical.

I want to remember the touch of a five-year-old who does not like to cuddle, the perfect feel of him as he climbs, of his own volition, into my arms. I want to remember how a tiny girl says, "Dance with me, Grandma," and the way she stomps and wiggles and spins while holding my hand, and for a moment I forget to be sad. I want to remember that a little boy draws his grandpa about to jump in a glacial pool. And draws him naked. Of course.

And I want to remember the sound of days upon days of laboured breath punctuated by a baby's shrieks and chuckles and "Patty Cake" and "Zoom, Zoom, Zoom." I want to remember that this is how it should be, all of it together, beginnings and endings, innocence and experience. I think that for the first time I understand the poetry of William Blake, glimmers of understanding that wink on and off. Maybe I do.

I want to remember the whole, rich, hard mess of this, that the worst moments are the ones of feeling nothing, that the best are in memory and in tears that turn to laughter and in laughter that turns to tears, and nothing is easy, not kindness nor grief nor love nor joy. It is all hard. And I think, *Is that the right word? "Hard"? Maybe it's "work."*

Work. Yes. It is all work. A lifetime's work—love and kindness and grief and joy and gratitude. We practise and we practise and it is work.

And what of grace? Is grace a simple, pure, exquisite moment when it is not work, it is not hard? Grace? In the midst of all the mess? That is as it should be. I think that is as it should be. I think so.

If I pray for anything, it is for eyes to see, for heart to hear the beauty and the thrumming song of grace. I want to remember . . . in his living and in his dying . . . he gave me this.

———————

The scarf is old and weary, clearly past its prime but still service-able—a bit like its owner. It bears the scars of a too-hot iron, and tiny pinpricks in the tartan testify to the presence of hungry moths at some point in its history. I've given up darning the moth holes. There are too many to count, but they are easily seen when I hold it up to the light.

Once upon a time it was a gift to mark the sad unravelling of a seven-year relationship, a gift from a man who was not the one for me—nor I for him—but who was generous to the end. It was, as the ads read, of the finest cashmere, patterned in the iconic Burberry plaid of camel, red, black, and white. It went with a camel hair coat, also a gift from him. I wore them both for years, the only time in my life that people have ever stopped me on the street to compliment me on my taste in outerwear. His taste, really. The coat disappeared from my life a long time ago, but I kept the scarf.

There is nothing more lovely to wrap around your neck than cashmere—light and soft, with all the warmth of other wools, but with none of the itchiness that even lamb's wool can generate. One winter Lincoln discovered it and fell in love with it, and I was forced to share. He knew its history, but it was now very old history, and jealousy was not in his nature.

The scarf was around my neck, however, on a late fall afternoon as we sat in the Vancouver airport with Sarah. She was leaving us to go to Kenya to work for a small NGO. She was a little teary and a little apprehensive, and I was desperate to model cheerfulness, to send her off with a smile and with the knowledge that we were confident in her ability to handle whatever came her way. The truth is we were, but how could she know that if I was weeping, too? When her flight was called, she looked at me, eyes huge and brimming in her beautiful face. I unwrapped the scarf from around my neck and rewrapped it around hers.

"There," I said. "I'm going with you, sweetheart."

That made her laugh.

"It's hot there!" she protested.

"Just for the plane, Sar," I said. "For comfort. It won't take up much room."

"It smells like you, Mom."

She grabbed her pack and headed through the gate without a backward look. She seemed so small, too young, though she had a university degree and a stint in Israel working on an archaeological project under her tiny belt. She had long dark hair and her father's gorgeous brown eyes. She was beautiful, smart, and kind. And she was deceptively tough, just like her dad. She still is all of those things. Lincoln and I walked silently back to the car and then I started to cry. Lincoln says I cried all the way to Princeton. That's three hours. He may have been right.

Sarah returned from Kenya in early summer, just in time for Naomi's high school graduation. We had been in touch as much as possible via email, but the stories she told in person made me realize how much her father's daughter she had become. She had grown up with the Kilimanjar Jar on the fridge, and her dad had taken her sister and her on innumerable hiking, biking, and backcountry skiing adventures. Of course she climbed Mount Kenya, though that was not in the plan when she left, not that I knew of, anyway. It was no small feat that she made it to the summit of the second-highest peak in Africa, smaller than Kilimanjaro by just a few hundred metres. I'm sure she knew how proud and happy the thought of her on the mountaintop made her father.

"I wore every piece of clothing I had with me," she told us while I shuddered and Lincoln beamed.

"And your scarf, Mom!" she said. "Your scarf saved me! I wrapped it around my face and head and tucked the ends down my chest for warmth. When Dad climbs Kilimanjaro he has to take the scarf."

And he did. On the climb that almost killed him, Lincoln wore the scarf. When I look at the photo, the one of him standing alone by the sign at the top of Uhuru Peak, my heart breaks all over again for what he must have gone through. He stands to one side of the sign, too tired and sick to lift his head for the camera. He looks beaten. But he isn't. And the scarf is around his neck, a bright flag in the dark, its tail ends catching the wind.

Early in Lincoln's illness, I turned to the Alzheimer Society of British Columbia for information and support. Julie, their support worker in the Kootenays, became an invaluable resource for me and many of us in Grand Forks who were struggling with caregiving. It was on their website that I first learned about the difference between Alzheimer's disease and Lewy body dementia. When I read in an email that they were sending a fundraising team up Kilimanjaro, my first thought was that I wished Lincoln could go. Or I could go. Then out of the blue, late one night, it hit me. The proverbial thunderbolt. The great idea. You know the kind, the ones that seem so brilliant at midnight and so regrettable by the light of day.

I can blame it on the Parkinson's meds, I thought in the morning. *I will tell them I was just wondering, writing it down to see if it made any sense. I never meant to hit Send. I will tell them levodopa can make people act impulsively. And I'm sorry to have bothered them. That's what I'll say.*

But before I could get my retraction written and sent, the response came.

"Yes! We'd love to send your scarf up the mountain, Leslie. We love its story. What a great idea! The scarf can go as an independent climber, with its own fundraising page, just like our other participants."

And so the Burberry scarf went up Kilimanjaro one more time. Every member of the Climb for Alzheimer's team took a turn wearing it. Every one of them climbed to honour someone they had lost or were losing to Alzheimer's. They all made it to the top, including the scarf. Thanks to the generosity of my friends and family, the Burberry scarf raised over three thousand dollars.

In the last winter of his life, I wrapped the scarf around my husband's neck every time I took him outside.

When I wear it now, I wrap it around my own neck and breathe deeply. Even though Parkinson's has eroded my sense of smell, I imagine I can still find Lincoln in its folds. And when I hold it up to the light, I don't see moth holes in the tiny pinpricks in the fabric. I see stars.

———————

On my way to the mail today I meet a dear friend who is home for two days between adventures. The last one took her away for less than a week; the next will take her and her husband away for three months. They will travel in a vw Westie named Goldie. Kindred spirits. I thought we had said goodbye for now, so this is serendipity.

And then suddenly Sarah is there and I get to talk for a bit with our girl, who waits for me to pick up my mail so she can drive me home. In the mailbox I find the newspaper and three parcel cards.

One parcel is from the final documents service to which I have subscribed. The purpose is to simplify the process of notifying all the many agencies and organizations that must be informed when someone dies. I am grateful for the help with all of this. I will look at it tomorrow.

The second, a mysterious, cylindrical-shaped parcel from high school friends who live in Ottawa, contains the perfect water bottle. It is sleek and made of stainless steel and is adorned with a photo of a mountain lake and a red canoe, in fact, four red canoes. One for each grandchild, I think to myself. The card that accompanies it can be planted—to grow a Lincoln tree, my friend says.

The third is from a friend I have never met, Laura, who illustrated *In the Red Canoe*. It contains two beautiful large gifts—I had no idea they would be so big, big enough to get lost in, or get found in—original paintings for the book. One is the night scene that graces the cover; the other is of Grandpa and child on the first pages. I cannot wait to frame them and hang them up. One day I will look at them without weeping, I know, but for now I am content to look at that watery world through watery eyes and think how very blessed I am—for this kindness, for all the book means to our family, for all the kindnesses and love that flow our way from so many directions.

How will I ever say thank you big enough? How will I ever pay it forward?

I find evenings especially hard, but every night after I close my book and turn out the light, I ask myself, *What was the gold this day?* Sometimes I wade through cynicism or sorrow and sometimes I pretend I have an answer, but I always do it. I don't think it as trivial a practice as it might sound.

We are into another summer of heat and fires. They are becoming as predictable as the changing seasons. The news is scary and the smoke in our valley is thick and distressing, and I almost talked myself out of going for the mail today, but the small act of walking to the post office brought to me a wide, clear world of goodness. Today's gold.

This is how the sleep goes: good night, bad night, good night, good night, bad night, bad night, good night badgoodgoodbad-badgoodgood . . . and nothing seems to really make a difference except half of a little blue pill, which has to be taken at exactly the right time or it wears off too early and I am awake at 4:00 AM, or it wears off too late and I find myself fighting to surface at 9:00 AM and the day, even before my first cup of coffee, seems already too warm for anything. I have to take a fistful of pills every day and I really, truly hate the thought of relying on another, so I am getting used to the pattern, or lack of pattern. As long as good finds its way in, say, one out of three, I think, *Okay, I can do this*.

The thing about the middle of the night is that I imagine I can smell smoke in the air. I can hardly smell anything, ever. Sense of smell disappears early in the progression of Parkinson's disease, but at 2:00 AM this nose of mine picks up the scent of woodsmoke from forests burning hundreds of kilometres away—forests, and farms, and houses, and the treasures and labours of lifetimes. The wildfire map on my computer screen assures me that nothing burns in our valley or too near; the smoke is drift from other people's loss, not ours, and it is reaching all the way to Saskatchewan.

The thing about the middle of the night is that all the worries of the daytime grow large, fed on dark and stillness and whatever else the night brings to, or steals from, the rational part of my brain. The thing about the middle of the night is that grief grows large, larger, largest, in waves and stabs and shifts. It dances with anxiety, and that is one hell of an unsettling, hobbling two-step.

And then there is the dawn, no matter the sleep or lack of it. Morning comes with all its must-dos or what-ifs and haze or sunrise glow, and somehow even the crows' raucous calling seems like better news than the midnight worries. Mourning comes, too, calm now, a waltz of memory, a slow, sorrowful pirouette on an unfamiliar—or is it too familiar?—stage. But that's not all. On the way home from yoga, my left foot quits on me. My fault. I forgot to take my meds, missed a dose. This is only the second time this has happened outside of my home. Not the missing the dose, that happens sometimes, too many times, but the foot supination thing. My left foot rolls onto its outside edge and my big toe stands up at a right angle to the ball of my foot. It hurts like hell and I cannot walk. At home, I can temporarily trick my brain by crawling. That will give me a few minutes of normal gait. The first time it happened outside was on a hike with friends when I mucked up my meds by eating too much protein too close to pill time. But this time I am alone, walking in the rising heat of a summer morning, just blocks from home and carrying a large box of twenty copies of my book that I have just picked up at the post office.

"It's heavy," the clerk said. "Do you have your car?"

"No, but I live close."

"Not that close."

"I'll be fine," I said, and I laughed to show her I was, I would be.

Half a block later, I am not fine. I sit down on the curb on a side street, grateful there is no traffic, no witnesses to my embarrassment, not yet, anyway. There really is no going forward and I just can't get my head around crawling. It would make for a good story, though. I take my pill, without water, because I'm not carrying water because I had planned to take my pill with the filtered, cold water at the yoga studio. It is a being-stupid kind of day.

I text the girls: *R U home?*

And while I wait—an oldish woman in not-very-chic yoga gear, sitting on the curb of a downtown side street with a cardboard box beside her and a cloth shopping bag in her lap—two young women, friends of one of our girls, walk by. They express concern. I tell them the simple version: missed my meds, took my meds, just waiting for the brain-to-foot conversation to get back on the rails. It won't be long. I tell my story cheerfully.

"I've got mail to read while I wait," I say.

I am convincing and they walk on. I talk to Lincoln, tell him where I am and what I am doing, and I hear him chuckle. He would love listening to me tell him how I crawled around on some stranger's lawn. It makes me wish I were. I pull my mail out of the bag, cards mostly, sympathy cards, bearing messages of love and understanding. I want to tell every kind writer, right then, where I am and what I am doing, and then listen to the collective chuckle.

And as I type this, I can feel my foot shift, rolling onto its outside edge. Damn. Ouch and damn. I check my watch. I missed my last pill.

On the next sleepless night, when I smell smoke, when the bizarre party starts inside my head, I am going to imagine that I am sitting on that curb, awash in kindness. I'll talk to Lincoln and we'll laugh. I might even try crawling on the lawn.

———————

I spend time each week with a wise teacher. She specializes in the wounded, those of us dealing with injury and pain. We work on breath and mindfulness, on discovering where and what our bodies hold on to and how to let go, how to find balance, how to know ourselves. I first sought her expertise in order to better manage my Parkinson's. Her practice helps with symptoms, amazingly so. I am less crooked, much less dizzy, in significantly less pain. She has an Australian's sense of humour, a little sarcastic, a little tart, thank goodness . . . and an empathetic heart. And she is smart, so smart.

This is what I learned from her: you can trick your mind but not your body. She rephrases it in the words of one of her mentors: What the mind suppresses, the body expresses. Yep.

Eight days after Lincoln died I went to her. She gently coached me through familiar, small movements. I was in someone else's skin, tense and jerky. Tight. Unable to find any ease or comfort. She asked me to lie down on my back. I knew she would watch how my breath flowed in and out. She spends a lot of time just watching. I get that. I spent a lot of my working life watching five-year-olds. The watching helped me understand where they were, how they were, and what they needed from me. Watching made me a better teacher. I think it is the same for her.

I could feel it before I knew it, the crack in my being, like the hair-thin fracture in the earth's crust that becomes a fissure, a widening crevasse, a tectonic shift, an earthquake splitting me down the middle, expressed in sobs that came from the pit of sadness, through the layers formed in years of grieving. And I wailed and howled while she held me, without touch or words, in the safety of her presence and in that space.

There are many things that surprise me about this new life of mine. That howling surprised me. I understand what people might mean when they say "out of body." I could no more have suppressed that cracking wide open than I could stand against the tide, but in the midst of those overwhelming waves of emotion, a dispassionate other-me quietly watched, quietly listened, astonished, a little bemused.

"What the heck?!" she said.

And "What the heck?!" one more time when it was over, when I stood up, lighter and stronger, back in my skin.

I am surprised by how much I miss Lincoln. After six years of losing him little by little, how can it be that I miss him so much now, when most of our life together was lost to me ages ago? What the heck?!

I am surprised by the ordinariness of my days, the getting up and doing stuff, by not spending every moment dripping tears, by laughing and forgetting to be sad, by talking aloud to him and talking to others about him, and not talking about him, and staying on my feet and being normal in a world that feels so very odd and so very familiar at the same time.

I am surprised, almost every day, by someone who loved him, too, and what they remember, the stories they tell, the Lincoln they knew, and the sense of loss they are experiencing. It comes in emails and cards and phone calls and conversations, face to face. And the words repeat. They name him: gentle, quiet, adventurous, unique, quirky, funny, iconoclastic, determined. Loved, loved you, loved by you, loved his family, loved his friends, loved his valley, loved the outdoors, loved to play. And those who knew him best, especially through these last few years, speak and write of his smile, and his courage, and his grace. And everyone has a memory or many, a story or ten to tell. And they don't place him on any pedestal, except the only pedestal he would ever want to be on, an unsteady resting place, one defined by his love of risk and his playful spirit. Lincoln never wasted his time wondering or worrying what others might think about him. That was a huge part of his attractiveness, that ability to be wholly himself, to live wholly in the moment. He enjoyed hearing that another Lincoln story was in circulation; he got a kick out of his small-town fame, or perhaps infamy is a better word. He saved trees, built trails, campaigned for environmental causes and against the banning of books, picked up garbage—everywhere, all the time—never saw the point of a bathing suit, took thousands of photographs, and was so often late I learned to lie about the time we were expected places. He loved movies, music, non-fiction books, and *Rolling Stone* magazine. He enjoyed a cold beer at the end of a hot hike but seldom drank any other alcohol, much preferring a joint smoked with a pal or two, under a star-blazed midnight sky. He worked hard, played harder, danced with his eyes closed, and liked to smooch on the chairlift. He made me crazy and proud and happy. I wish he were here.

A book came today in the mail, sent by a friend who knows an unimaginable sorrow. It is short meditations on grief. Short is good, my mind having become a frantic gerbil. Already I have been surprised and comforted by words that better express what I struggle to say. Thornton Wilder, the preface tells me, said, "The greatest tribute to the dead is not grief but gratitude."[3] Gratitude. There's that word again.

And the first short meditation speaks of tenderness, in all its meanings, as the natural state of grief.

Yesterday I spoke with a friend and used the word "tender" to describe how I felt. I am grateful to be on the same page as the writer. We all are, or will be. Right? We all wear our losses like bruises. We touch them, however tenderly, and they hurt. And that pain tells us that we loved. I don't doubt that there are howling times to come, and I wonder if this gets easier, ever. But if someone had told me I would get through losing him the way I did, I would not have believed it possible, never would have believed it possible. It didn't get easier but we got through it—my girls and I—whatever through means. It does not mean "over."

It is just this day, one day, and if we are lucky there might be a wise teacher, or a memory, or a friend. There will be breath in, breath out, breaking apart and mending. Just this day. Again and again.

What I wish for myself, I wish for all of us—words that comfort, hope that guides, and love to hold us in its gaze.

―――――――――――

In the photograph he is dressed in jeans and a T-shirt. In one hand he is holding a snake stick and in the other a rattlesnake, as thick as his upper arm and almost as long as he is tall, hanging beaded tail down. And he is grinning.

Lincoln loved rattlesnakes. He found them fascinating and thrilling. During the years we lived in Grand Forks, he hiked many times up to their dens. He picked them up to get a closer look and took hundreds of photographs and hours of video, all within fang-strike range. He was fearless. People talked about how brave he was. And he was—but I don't think it was revealed by his adventures with snakes. Courage is what you demonstrate when you face things that freak the hell out of you. That's what I think. His love of snakes did not mean that he was brave. It did make him famous, though, in a small-town way. As for his courage, he taught me lessons in courage that I will never be able to master, but they have nothing to do with snakes.

The "snake whisperer," one friend called him. Every summer, when the rattlesnakes found their way down from their overheated dens to the valley bottom and well-watered, shady backyards, he would get phone calls.

"There's a rattler in my garden!" a panicked voice would cry.

Lincoln would head out, armed with one of his snake-catching sticks, forked at one end for pinning the head. The trick, he would tell you, is to hold the snake right at the base of its head. The back of its head. And hold it tight. He had a collection of five-gallon commercial mayonnaise containers with lids that fit snugly and were hard to remove. He used these to transport the snakes. He would seal a captured snake in a container, pack it upriver away from town, then somehow remove the lid and fling the snake out into the water. He claimed they were good swimmers, that they always headed in the right direction, that they never turned around and headed back toward him. I don't know how he managed any of it, how he removed those tricky lids and tossed the snakes without being bitten. I never went with him. I am terrified of snakes. The smallest garden-variety kind sets my heart to banging against my ribs so fiercely that I must hold it in place by pressing on my chest with both hands. I am not fearless.

One spring, for a school-wide science fair, Lincoln brought two big rattlers down from the dens and set them up in an aquarium in the school library. He rationalized that he wanted to show them to the kids so they would recognize both the look and the sound of the snakes if they encountered them in the bush. He wanted them to see how beautiful they were. It also guaranteed a steady stream of visitors to his library. I was horrified by the risk he had taken and was angry with him. I was sure he had crossed a line. I was not alone, though the protest came not from parents or even the district administration but from provincial officialdom. A uniformed game warden showed up at our door that evening and chewed him out for messing with a protected species and demanded that the snakes be returned to their natural habitat. I don't think he could have known that those snakes would be transported home as they had been transported to town—in a plastic pail strapped by bungee cords to the back of Lincoln's mountain bike. The trail to the dens was narrow, steep, and rocky, challenging enough for a skilled cyclist unencumbered, never mind one with venomous, angry reptiles at his back.

It isn't until years later, at the celebration of life we hold for Lincoln, that I learn he also had been ordered to pay a hefty fine.

"He told me about the fine and asked me not to tell you," our former principal tells me as he says goodbye.

He shakes his head as he speaks, and he chuckles. There are a lot of stories told that afternoon. There is a lot of head shaking. A lot of chuckling.

In the early morning on the day of Lincoln's party, his celebration of life, I walk the paved section of our local greenbelt. I want time to myself, to let tears fall, and to compose a tranquil, public face to wear. I find myself thinking about bears. I'm not afraid of bears the way I am of snakes, but it is early autumn and early morning, and I am alone on the path, without any noisemakers or bear spray. I don't think my cellphone will be of much use if an encounter with Yogi turns sour.

Then this happens all at once: not a bear but two young men on skateboards whiz around a curve straight toward me, and a garter snake slithers out of the grass and across the path, almost at my feet. I freeze.

"Snake!" I screech.

One skateboarder slips by me on one side. The other jumps off, flips up his board, and catches it in his hands, deftly avoiding both me and the snake.

"Just a little guy," he says.

Then they all disappear, the snake in a few quick twitches and the young men in a chatter of wheels. I hear a faint cry of "Snake!" echoing from around the next bend. And then laughter.

"Oh, buddy," I scold. "Not funny!"

Later that same day about sixty of us, family and friends, gather. It is a day washed clean and clear of smoke and that awful, oppressive, our-world-is-burning dread. It is a day of weeping skies, a day when, surely, the earth softens and sighs with sweet relief.

I worry about all the people travelling from far away to be with us, about all the goodness and kindness and unselfishness I can never return in kind. There is too much and they are too many. I worry about what they might need from our party and hope they will find it here, with us, this day.

Two good men, John and Chris, speak about Lincoln, speak their sorrow and their joy and their wisdom and their honesty, and, mostly, their friendship. I repeat their words with their permission. They talk about the stories, the many, many stories. They both acknowledge the Lincoln legends and know they will be shared in conversations that day and in the days to come, but they don't tell stories. They speak instead about the impact of his life on theirs.

Chris says:

I hear Lincoln in the quiet ripples and splash of the creek racing over an edge on its way to somewhere. I can hear his voice telling me that we are also close to some unknown destination. It's just over the next hill . . . around the next bend . . . it's easy from here . . . When your purpose was to get lost, you could always count on Lincoln. And we all wanted to get lost. We wanted to explore the amazing landscape and fly down hillsides on mountain bike wings. Moonlight skiing turned us into fairy kings in a sparkling universe. Kayaking the impatient cold white waters brought us face to face with our own mortality. And always there was the forest to worship. The strength and dignity and life force in some old snag was never lost on Lincoln. He was literally a tree hugger and would hug and comfort those twisted wooden beasts. And just like him I have come to worship the forest we live with. The forest is truly magical and

strong and powerful with a life force that can only be observed from deep within its mysterious places. That is where you are when you are truly lost.

But he could invariably get you home too. I don't know how he did it, but he always knew the way.

And from John, this:

I loved the outdoors and doing adventures—but these were serious well-planned adult adventures. However, Lincoln taught me how to play as an adult—to abandon the seriousness of what we do and just focus on the fun of the adventure. After a few exhilarating invigorating playful adventures I happily joined up to be one of the Lost Boys. Lincoln knew about the importance of play years before it became talked about in educational and professional settings. The playing I did with Lincoln helped change my views of the world—my heart became lighter and a smile was more frequently on my face. I thank him for that and, as a devoted follower, I firmly believe we

should all spend much more time playing.

Of course there was more to Lincoln than laughter and play. He was a quiet man. I spent a great deal of time with him without many words being spoken—once I learned to be quiet! We shared a similar connection to nature—we were both comfortable and relaxed out in the natural world. And while we climbed many peaks in adrenalin-filled exhilaration, there was always something special about the journey down/home.

It was often a time of quiet reflection and introspection as we embraced the natural beauty of our surroundings in silence. We were in awe—words weren't needed.

In recent years as Lincoln started down the road to dementia, I was amazed by his gentle acceptance of his predicament. Yes, he got frustrated—very frustrated by newly discovered limitations or his inability to vocalize his thoughts coherently. But he never held on to the frustration and allowed it to turn to bitterness. Rather he gracefully accepted the reality of his new and much altered life.

Both Chris and John give clear-eyed, loving honour to one of their own, the Lost Boy whose wandering, narrowing path took him away from them, and all of us. And hard as it has been, these long years of losing him, they have always held him in their sights, held him close. I listen to them and think how much of who we are is measured by who loves us. He is measured large. He was loved by the best of friends.

My extraordinary sister Jane reads aloud the poem I wrote and tucked in Lincoln's backpack when he left for his Paris-to-Istanbul bike trip. It's not a great poem but she makes it seem beautiful, while my other extraordinary sister, Margaret, holds me close and lends me her strength.

Our daughters make a list—a poster to be quietly read by our guests—that tells the many ways their father showed his love and the many things they learned from him. Like me, neither of them feels able to speak about him with any measure of self-control. They were, they are, the centre of his universe. They saw him with eyes much clearer than mine, much of the time.

All of it, enough words, perfect words, not too many words for my man of few words.

And a slide show of Chris's making, to tell the story in photographs of a life well lived, enviably well lived, well lived and well loved, from first breath to last. Unplanned and unbidden, we find ourselves singing "Rise Again" as his story unfolds in pictures in front of us.

Later, our friends' lovely voices surround the baby, Maisie, sitting plopped on her tiny bottom, blue eyes taking each singer in by turn. Soul to soul. Enchantment.

There are hugs and tears and laughter and old friends and new. And women, my women, my sisters, my friends. The grandkids play, in and out, sweet and happy. We are touched by the grace of all who come in person. We feel the presence of those who come in spirit. We rise again.

Our Dad

Important Things Our Dad Taught Us:

Shoe Goo can fix anything.

If you take care of your stuff, it will last forever.

You can never have too many rolled up plastic bags in your backpack.

If you're sad, go for a walk. If you're really sad, go for a hike.

Never let lack of proper gear stop you from going on an adventure.

If skiing, walking, or swimming is feeling a bit dull, try it with your eyes closed.

Find a quiet moment with CBC Radio every day.

How to maximize the carrying capacity of any dish-drying rack, any car-top carrier, or any vehicle.

You can never have too many bungee cords.

An ample stockpile of dried fruit is always necessary.

Never ever walk or drive by a piece of litter.

How to go through life doing what's important to you, instead of saying what's important to you.

How to be quietly brave in the face of daunting personal obstacles and how to make everyone else feel brave as well.

Dad showed us that he loved us, in a million tiny ways, every day, by:

Sharing his secret chocolate stash midway through a hike, especially when there are three more hours to go.

Handing us little bowls of frozen peas and peeled carrots while we set the table before dinner.

Immediately washing and vacuuming our cars every time
we came home from university.

Giving us each a single rose every Valentine's Day.

Offering a slice of anything he was eating, even if it was
just a hunk of cabbage.

Always welcoming a couch snuggle while he watched his
pre-recorded 6:00 PM news.

Bringing us fruit in bed, early morning or late at night,
whether we wanted it or not.

Packing and unpacking our lives, for every ski trip,
camping trip, or vacation.

Winking at us during any sort of serious meeting, so that
we would get the giggles.

Puttering and pacing around the house, even if he wanted to
go to bed, just so he could be the one to lock the door, turn
out the lights, and make sure we were safe in bed.

Offering to take us on every adventure, walk, hike, or ski.

Buying any groceries we wanted as long as we wrote it on
the list.

Letting us pre-read all the new books from the Hutton
library.

Cutting out and keeping every single newspaper clipping
about either of us.

Documenting our entire lives in endless photographs and
on video.

Having just enough Werther's Originals in his pocket to
share with us, and pretending it was a fluke that he had just
the right number to go around.

Always making us think we could accomplish anything we
wanted.

Every fall, I used to read a picture book called *Rain Makes Applesauce* to my kindergarten students. I never owned my own copy. It came from the Hutton School library, Lincoln's library. It was a funny, quirky, offbeat little book with the nonsensical refrain "You're just talking silly talk!"[4] And it was always a hit.

I think of it as it rains and I make applesauce. Applesauce is not supposed to be my job; it was Lincoln's, and this is the first time I've made it on my own. It's not that it is difficult—it isn't—but getting motivated and staying motivated to cook for myself has been a struggle ever since he went into care. Remembering the book makes me smile; then it makes me feel old, as the memories seem so long ago. I bought all these apples at the farmers' market because they looked so beautiful. And I love applesauce. And it is raining. Reason enough, I suppose.

As I chop and mash and stir and round up jars and lids, to the back sound of the rain, I remember all the times we worked together in the kitchen, Lincoln, me, and CBC. I talk to the radio and I talk to him. He mostly listens.

"You know they can't hear you," he says. "The voices on the radio can't hear you."

"But you can!"

"I can," he says and laughs.

"If you want me to be quiet, I can be."

And that makes him laugh again. It is our shtick. For no one else but him and me. Old-married-couple's shtick. I miss it. His cooking style is tidy and efficient, well planned, librarian-ish. Mine is chaotic and often interrupted by the need for a trip to the grocery store for a missing ingredient.

"I'll go," he says, almost always.

Grocery shopping is his job. It doesn't become mine until he needs help. When the time comes when he can no longer go alone, I discover the goodness of the people who work at our local grocery store, the cashiers who patiently coach him through the steps for using his debit card, who wait while he insists on bagging his own groceries, who leave the till to find the things he can't find himself. Department managers make a point of coming over to talk to us, and teenaged kids who'd been his students, and have part-time jobs filling shelves, greet him.

"Hi, Mr. Ford," they say.

Sometimes they turn to me and tell me how his library was a haven for them or how he showed up in their classrooms with books, newly catalogued, that he knew they would like, that he had purchased with them in mind. They tell me how that made them feel.

They remember the Friday field trips. His goal was to get them out of the school every Friday afternoon, and he came close to doing that. Lincoln and his kids and a few parents roamed the valley and the hills, even visiting the rattlesnake dens. He showed his kids where they lived. He taught them the meaning of home. And as they tell their memories, everyone holds their sorrow and their honouring in their gentleness with him, and in their eyes.

When it comes time to put the apple mash through the food mill, I discover it is a job for two well-behaved hands. On the best day, I've got one reasonably obedient hand and one brat. I settle on a system that involves hugging the bowl while I turn the handle on the mill. To the accompaniment of some moments of involuntary parkie dancing, I manage to get some applesauce through the mill and into the bowl, and the rest on me, the counter, and the floor.

At one point, close to tears with frustration and the melancholy of the rain and the missing of him, I take a break. This appears on a friend's Facebook page. It is a poem, "Epitaph" by Merrit Malloy, and is included in the Reform Jewish prayer book as an option before reading more traditional forms of liturgy. I love these lines:

> Look for me in the people I've known or loved,
> and if you cannot give me away,
> at least let me live in your eyes and not in your mind.
> You can love me best by letting hands touch hands,
> and by letting go of children that need to be free.
> Love doesn't die, people do.
> So, when all that's left of me is love,
> give me away.[5]

"Let me live in your eyes and not in your mind." Oh boy. I'm not there yet, not able to do that yet. Lincoln lives so very much in my mind. I don't know if, or when, I will be able to give him away, but I hold that place and time in possibility, in gratitude, and in wonder.

Rain makes applesauce and rain makes kitchen shtick. Such a perfect little non sequitur leading to such perfect and tender and bittersweet places . . . to touching hands and giving to others what I need to give him and to remembering what others have given to us. And to letting go and to the sureness of love that doesn't die.

Postlude

WE HAVE COME BACK to the town where Lincoln and I took our ten-month-old baby girl, to the town where four years later her little sister was born.

We always imagined we would find ourselves old, Lincoln and I, in that little town, the one where the rivers meet, where the north-facing hills rise covered in fir and larch, and the south-facing hills bake summer-grass golden, and solitary ponderosa pines cling to rock and crumbling earth.

We are here this weekend to scatter Lincoln's ashes, to give him to a river that tumbles out of a high mountain watershed and winds its way through old-growth forest before it seeks the valley bottom, a river loved by all of us, but loved with a full-heartedness beyond telling by him.

We gather on a sandy beach one morning, a small group of family and beloved friends-who-are-family, and we cast silver-grey ashes to the air and to the water. They shimmer luminous in the sunlight and swirl in opalescent patterns in the river. We are quiet but not silent; we hug one another and weep and laugh and speak to him in private whispers or in no words at all. Then the little ones discover the maze of beach trails and we watch another generation find noisy joy in that treasured river shore.

I look for something—a bird, a butterfly, perhaps a coyote slipping along the far bank, a shape in a cloud, something I can imagine, if only for a moment, speaks to his presence. I feel a little foolish in my regret that nothing appears. It is, however, a place to stir memories, and as we climb back up to the main trail, we talk of summers past.

Okay, I tell myself, *he is here, in this place, in our stories. It's okay. He's here.*

We go as far as the trail takes us, to a lookout high above the river, a precipitous drop-off where the remnants of a long-abandoned dam have witnessed Lincoln-legend canoe and kayak misadventures. We clutch our little people by the hand and let them peek over the edge before retreating to the safety of the path. As we wander back, I grow rueful once more, greedy for comfort. I want symbol and magic, a wish to come true.

Even a cranky old crow will do, I think to myself. *But no snakes!*

On our return journey, we meet old friends who are biking toward us on the trail.

"Did you see the eagle?" they ask.

And they turn around to lead us to him.

He is resting, almost at eye level and unperturbed by our presence, in a sapling on our side of the river. He is close, astonishingly close. As we watch him, he gazes, for a long time, one way up the river and then the other, that majestic white head and beak presenting a perfect profile.

Take your time, he seems to say, as if he knows how beautiful he is, what he means to us.

"Hey," I tell him. "There you are."

"Hey, Dad. Late again," Sarah says.

He glances our way once, and only briefly, before rising and settling on a new perch, farther away.

As we walk above the beach where we spread his ashes, we can still see those swirls in the water, fainter now, like inverse shadows, gossamer tracings. They will not be there for long, nor visible anywhere. Yet he is present, mingled with the river, drifting in the wind, gleaming for a moment in an eagle's hooded eye.

Home. He is home, wherever he is and everywhere he is. If I choose to believe it. And I choose.

> I will be bound to my man of the hills
> I will watch his star from the lower ridge
> The canoe will carry us both ashore
> The road will bear us onward still
> His eyes will shine in a small boy's face
> And tender sunset blessings grace
> This bittersweet will be will be
> And tethered are we to we.

Acknowledgements

DANCING IN SMALL SPACES had its formal beginning in January 2018, in the studio designed by architect Ian Davidson (no relation) in the Leighton Artist Studios at the Banff Centre for Arts and Creativity. I wrote every day for ten cold, snowy days, and the end result was a lot of stutter writing—many starts, many stops—and the first three pages of the book. That works out to about 180 usable words a day. But writing, I told myself, was a practice, and I thank CBC Books, the Canada Council for the Arts, and the Banff Centre for this amazing, humbling, inspiring opportunity to practise. A portion of this memoir first appeared on CBC Books as "Adaptation."

Good teachers and mentors, whether the student is a five-year-old in a kindergarten classroom or a seventy-year-old trying to tell a story of love and loss, know the best work is created in a climate of safety and trust, through gentle counsel, wise example, and encouragement. I met the author Becky Blake over breakfast on my first morning in Banff. She joins other generous, talented writers who have offered that gentle counsel, wise example, and encouragement.

I also owe a debt of gratitude to: Jenna Butler for advice and encouragement provided through the blue pencil workshop at the Elephant Mountain Literary Festival, July 2021. Nellwyn Lampert for providing thoughtful editorial commentary. Sarah Selecky for the learning of the craft provided by her Story Is a State of Mind and Short Story Intensive online courses and the mentorship of Nicole Baute and Kristin Offiler. Kara Stanley for kindly reading a first draft and sharing it with her then-agent Carolyn Swayze. Both Kara and Carolyn made me feel I might have something worth sharing at a time of crippling self-doubt. Alison Wearing for cheerleading and answering questions and for honouring my writing by including it in her memoir-writing course.

As I write these names and hold these gifted, generous women in my heart, I realize my sister Jane Davidson is the remarkable tie that binds. In her role as the artistic and executive director of the Sunshine Coast Festival of the Written Arts, Jane knows Canadian writers and Canadian books. She pointed me in the direction of Sarah Selecky and introduced me to her friend Kara Stanley, and so to Carolyn Swayze. Jane suggested I read Alison Wearing's books, and Alison recommended Nellwyn Lampert. When Tori Elliott, acting publisher at TouchWood Editions, offered me a contract, Jane responded with "B and G [Brindle & Glass, an imprint of TouchWood Editions] publish beautiful books," and "Tori & Co. are good people." And indeed they do, and indeed they are. Tori took the risk on an aging first-time author and I thank her and returning publisher Taryn Boyd, copy editor Meg Yamamoto, proofreader Claire Philipson, designer Sydney Barnes, and my always-encouraging publicist, Curtis Samuel.

And that brings me to Kate Kennedy, my editor at Brindle & Glass, who has guided me through a series of revisions with respect and patience. Her gentle counsel, wise example, and encouragement have made this, I think, a much better book. It has been a challenge to meet her expectations but I am so grateful for the opportunity to try. There has been joy in the process, joy and laughter. That has been the best surprise. Kate, a thousand thank yous.

To the members of Writers' Bloc, my writing support group in Revelstoke, BC, Michelle Cole, Jenny Granville, Carolyn Johnston,

Tim Palmer, Poppi Reimer, and Laura Stovel, I am grateful for your friendship, and for your careful listening to every word I wrote. You asked the good, clarifying questions and responded with honest and considered opinions. I am so lucky to have you in my corner.

A loving circle of friends provided incomparable support from the time of our joint diagnoses in 2011 to Lincoln's death in 2017 and in the days that followed. I know that, no matter how many I list, I will leave off names that should be here. I apologize for the oversight. There are no words adequate to the task of thanking Jean Byrnell and Liz Mason, Jill and Dave Carson, Stephanie Cruit, Barb Dann and Steve Warren, Leora Gesser, Jude Kerr, Chris and Kathy Moslin, Robbin Thomson, and John and Mary Ann Westaway for all their practical and emotional support.

To Lorna Blatkewicz, Diana Carr and Ron Liddle, Donna Dobbie, Debra Dolan, Sue Dulley, Shawn Funk, Sally Garcelon, Tracey Garvin, Yvonne Gidney, Martin Gidney, Rachel Grav, Susan and Ted Harrison, Maria-Lynn Johnson and Marc Paradis, Neil Jones, Terry King, the late Christy Luke, Lee and Butch Macri, Melanie and David Merry, Jane and Bob Morton, Muriel Neale, Pete and Nancy Perry, Ronnie Ross, the late Gail Russell, Jon Stamford, Jane Usher, Lisa Vanderburg, Erika and Dan Von Bank, Josie Woodman, and Margot Wylie, thank you for many sustaining kindnesses. In an unforgettable expression of love and support, Lincoln's cousins, Graham and Yvonne Bushill, Maureen Harrison, and Rob Pimlott, all made the long trip from England in the summer of 2015 to visit Lincoln in his care facility, and to say goodbye.

To the staff at Hardy View Lodge in Grand Forks and Mount Cartier Court in Revelstoke, my heartfelt gratitude for embracing Lincoln and our family, and for doing your difficult jobs with compassion and skill. To Dr. Kate McCarroll of Selkirk Medical in Revelstoke, thank you for clarifying a few medical questions. I've tried to keep the science as simple and accurate as possible and take full responsibility for any misinformation. To my parkie tribe, sadly ever expanding, I honour your courage and resilience.

And to my family—my siblings, and siblings-in-law, Bill and Maion Davidson, Jane Davidson and Boyd Norman, and Margaret Davidson—you have been a sounding board, unfazed by my tears, open, generous, and an infinite source of unconditional love and, thank goodness, no small measure of goofiness and hilarity.

Lincoln and I were blessed with beautiful and good daughters who married kind, loving men. Isaac Becker and Jason Zimmer, thank you for your patience and support. Sarah and Naomi, your dad loved you beyond words and was so very proud of you. You have been staunch, joy-bringing presences in both of our lives, always. Thank you for trusting me to tell our story.

Our mountain babies, Arlo, Essey, Theron, Maisie, you light up my life! Maybe one day you will read these tales and get to know the grandfather in the red canoe, the soft-spoken adventurer whose courage and grace at his life's end remain his most profound legacy.

Speaking of Speaking

Readers may wonder how much creative licence I exercised as I wrote the dialogue in the book. The longer conversations between Lincoln and me were taken directly from emails, usually sent to my family. I wrote almost daily when phone conversations became impossible, so these are based on recall from the same day. I made notes of, and repeated to family and friends, many of Lincoln's comments because, despite the disease, he was often funny. We all needed the laughter. And some conversations were so poignant, so bittersweet, they are etched in my memory. None of the stories are inventions; all are as honest as memory permits. In some cases, the dialogue is more imagined than specifically recalled but, after so many years together, I can still hear our voices. I talk to him all the time.

Notes

1 "What Is Lewy Body Dementia? Causes, Symptoms and Treatments," National Institute on Aging, July 29, 2021, www. nia.nih.gov/health/what-lewy-body-dementia-causes-symptoms-and-treatments; "Science," Lewy Body Society, 2021, www.lewybody.org/about-lbd/science/.

2 Atul Gawande, *Being Mortal: Illness, Medicine and What Matters in the End* (London: Profile Books, 2014), 109.

3 Martha W. Hickman, *Healing After Loss: Daily Meditations for Working Through Grief* (New York: William Morrow, 1994). This book doesn't have page numbers; there are a year's worth of meditations. This quote is from the introduction, page x.

4 Julian Scheer, *Rain Makes Applesauce* (New York: Holiday House, 1964).

5 Merrit Malloy, "Epitaph." A concerted search has not turned up any contact information for Merrit Malloy or her publisher.

Resources

There are many, many organizations, Facebook pages, blogs, podcasts, books, and articles dedicated to the support of Parkinson's and dementia patients and caregivers, treatments, and research. I found the following helpful.

FOR PARKINSON'S DISEASE
Books

Dorsey, Ray, Todd Sherer, Michael S. Okun, and Bastiaan R. Bloem. *Ending Parkinson's Disease: A Prescription for Action.* New York: PublicAffairs, 2020.

Fox, Michael J. *A Funny Thing Happened on the Way to the Future: Twists and Turns and Lessons Learned.* New York: Hyperion, 2010.

Fox, Michael J. *Always Looking Up: The Adventures of an Incurable Optimist.* New York: Hyperion, 2009.

Fox, Michael J. *Lucky Man: A Memoir.* New York: Hyperion, 2002.

Fox, Michael J. *No Time Like the Future: An Optimist Considers Mortality.* New York: Flatiron Books, 2020.

Levy, Robyn. *Most of Me: Surviving My Medical Meltdown.* Vancouver: Greystone Books, 2012.

Palfreman, Jon. *Brain Storms: My Fight Against Parkinson's and the Race to Unlock the Secrets of One of the Brain's Most Mysterious Diseases.* Toronto: HarperCollins, 2015.

Podcasts

When Life Gives You Parkinson's: www.parkinson.ca/resources/when
-life-gives-you-parkinsons-presented-by-parkinson-canada/

Websites

Brian Grant Foundation: www.briangrant.org
Davis Phinney Foundation: www.davisphinneyfoundation.org
Michael J. Fox Foundation: www.michaeljfox.org
Parkinson Canada: www.parkinson.ca
Parkinson's Foundation: www.parkinson.org
Parkinson Society British Columbia: www.parkinson.bc.ca
Parkinson Wellness Projects: www.parkinsonwellness.ca
PD Avengers: www.pdavengers.com
World Parkinson Coalition: www.worldpdcoalition.org

FOR DEMENTIA
Books

Arden, Jann. *Feeding My Mother: Comfort and Laughter in the Kitchen as a Daughter Lives with Her Mom's Memory Loss.* Toronto: Penguin Random House Canada, 2019.

Borrie, Cathie. *The Long Hello: Memory, My Mother, and Me.* Toronto: Simon & Schuster Canada, 2015.

Leavitt, Sarah. *Tangles: A Story about Alzheimer's, My Mother, and Me.* Calgary: Freehand Books, 2010.

Martini, Clem, and Olivier Martini. *The Unravelling: How Our Caregiving Safety Net Came Unstrung and We Were Left Grasping at Threads, Struggling to Plait a New One.* Calgary: Freehand Books, 2017.

Podcasts

Fading Memories: www.fadingmemoriespodcast.com
What the Dementia: https://podcasts.apple.com/us/podcast
/what-the-dementia/id1494802478

Websites

Alzheimer Society of British Columbia: www.alzheimer.ca/bc/en
Alzheimer Society of Canada: www.alzheimer.ca/en
The Dementia Society: www.dementiahelp.ca
Family Caregivers of British Columbia: www.familycaregiversbc.ca
Lewy Body Dementia Association: www.lbda.org
The Lewy Body Society: www.lewybody.org/about-lbd/science/

PHOTO BY SARAH MICKEL PHOTOGRAPHY

Leslie A. Davidson is the author of two children's books, *In the Red Canoe* (2016) and *The Sun is a Shine* (2021). Her essay "Adaptation" won the CBC Canada Writes Creative Non-fiction Prize and her work has been published in the *Globe and Mail, Viewpoints, PostScript,* and *On the Move.* Davidson is a retired elementary school teacher, a mother, and grandmother. She lives in Revelstoke, BC. You can find her online at leslieadavidson.com.